(top) Headquarters of Russian secret police, near Metropole Hotel in Moscow. (bottom, left to right) Pushkin monument on main Moscow thoroughfare. Author as he appeared when he made the journey from Minneapolis to Moscow. Marie Petrovna and Homer Smith as he appeared during World War II when he covered Russian front as correspondent. Eleanor Ross, Wayland Rudd, Jr., and Inez Ross, children of American Negro expatriates.

BLACK MAN
IN RED RUSSIA

BLACK MAN
IN RED RUSSIA

A memoir

by

HOMER SMITH

with an introduction by

Harrison Salisbury

Johnson Publishing Company
Chicago · 1964

To

MARIE   PETROVNA

My Beloved Wife

•

To

CATHERINE   PUSHKIN

One of My Best Russian Friends

INTRODUCTION

One day in the winter of 1944 I was standing at the window of a Russian railroad car, watching the endless vista of snow, pine forests, birch groves and tamarack swamps flow by. It was mid-afternoon and in that northern latitude already the evening shadows had begun to gather.

Turning to my companion I said: "For all the world that countryside looks just like Minnesota—same trees, same landscape, same snow."

"That's a fact," he said, then added, a little surprised: "Are you from Minnesota?"

"Indeed, I am," I replied. "Where are you from?"

"Minnesota," he said and we both laughed. It seemed a long way to come—to a Russian train slowly moving northward across the battle-scarred land—to meet a fellow countryman.

The Minnesotan of that train ride was Homer Smith. Although neither of us had recognized the other in this strange and unexpected milieu we were not only fellow Minnesotans —we were fellow students at the University of Minnesota, had studied in some of the same classes and had even worked together on the student newspaper fifteen or sixteen years earlier.

Once out of the University our paths had separated. Now many years and many thousands of miles later they had once more crossed.

I saw a lot of Homer Smith in that year of 1944. We foreign correspondents lived together in the Metropole Hotel. We saw each other almost every day. Every week or so we would be off on a new trip to another part of Russia. The Red

Army was advancing, hurling back the Germans from Russian soil and the Foreign Office was eager to take the correspondents to the scenes of the latest Soviet victories.

The year of 1944 was a good one for learning about Russia. We saw more of the countryside and more Russian people than foreigners were to see for many years thereafter. There was an ease of communication, a camaraderie which was quickly to be lost in the reinstitution of Stalin's iron controls.

It was not hard to perceive that there was an amazing gap between the official version of life in the Soviet Union and the reality. But of the breadth and depth of this gap no one of the war-time correspondents could possibly have such precise and intimate knowledge as an observer such as Homer Smith who lived in Russia for almost a decade before the outbreak of war.

Homer Smith in this volume tells his own story and it needs no commentary. It is the straight-forward account of an American Negro's experience of Soviet reality. It is, in a sense, a story of the failure of a promise—and it was a real promise—which the Soviet held out in terms of complete absence of race prejudice (indeed, as he notes, the prejudice far from being "anti" was almost embarrassingly "pro") turned to ashes under the impact of the tyranny and lack of civil freedom within the system.

And this tragedy may even be understated in Homer Smith's book. He describes the almost instant surge of chauvinism and nationalism which accompanied the outbreak of World War II; the fierce suspicions; the quick intervention of the police against the foreigner—against any foreigner, in fact. This book tells a personal narrative. But it could be generalized to tell of the treatment of every kind of minority and foreigner in Russia during the terrible war-time days and thereafter.

Negroes were not the only minorities which had been attracted to Russia in the 1930's. There were radicals of many hues and many lands. There were the oppressed of many tyrannies. There were refugees from Spain and Communist Germans who had escaped Hitler.

For all of these there was short shrift in war-time Russia. If anything Homer Smith's account minimizes not only the treatment of these classes—but also his own difficulties. The war brought hard times to everyone in Russia—but the hardest times of all to those who before the war had enjoyed special consideration and even, as he observes, "pampered" treatment.

Stalin's purges were no respecters of race or nationality. The tragic story of the American Negro Communist, Lovett Forte-Whiteman, the "ideological" leader of the American Negro colony in Moscow who vanished in the 1937 purges, is here told, I believe, for the first time.

No less ironic is the story of Paul Robeson's brother-in-law, Frank Goode, now living out his declining days in the Russian provinces on the pension awarded him by the Soviet government after a lifetime spent in exhibiting his strength as a professional wrestler in Russian travelling circusses and carnivals.

The half-amusing, half-sad story of the great film venture of the early 1930's—the proposed Russian movie, Black and White, which would expose the viciousness of American racism and which foundered on the diplomatic realities of President Roosevelt's move to establish Soviet-American relations provides an instructive example of Soviet real politik. And it also contributed to the tragedy of the lives of several American Negroes who went to Russia for the picture and never regained their American homeland.

Homer Smith left Russia in 1946. He managed to get his Russian wife out of the country in 1947. He was a fortunate man, more fortunate than he indicates. Had he not managed to make his way to Ethiopia at that time he might well have encountered the fate of so many other foreigners who lived and worked in Russia—arrest, trial without judge or jury, the long sentence to Siberian labor camp or possibly death.

Soviet suspicion and paranoia deepened after he and his wife left. The position of the handful of Negroes remaining in the Soviet Union became even more precarious. They found it difficult to get jobs. The warmth and friendliness they had experienced earlier vanished in the grim atmosphere of Stalin's declining years.

In recent years another facet of the race question has emerged in Russia—the appearance of race prejudice directed against African students in the Soviet universities and institutes, a phenomenon which has led to serious incidents, including mass picketing and protests in Red Square.

To those who have known the Soviet well and who have been aware of the deep hold which nationalistic chauvinism possesses over the Great Russian people; who have heard the cliches of Russian anti-Semitic jokes; who have observed the customary condescension displayed toward the "subject" peoples of Central Asia; who have noted the sharp xenophobia displayed by Russians toward Poles or Chinese, the public manifestation of Russian antagonism toward Africans and peoples of dark skins comes as no real surprise.

Historically, the Russians had never had contact with peoples of Africa. There was, it is true, a tiny enclave of dark-skinned people long resident in the Caucasus, so-called Russian native Negroes. But few Russians had ever heard of them and not one in ten thousand had seen them. When the first American Negroes of contemporary times appeared in the Soviet in the late 1920's and early 1930's they were a curiosity beyond compare. In a land always starved for *exotica* (as the Russian phrase has it) these pleasant, different-appearing, different-speaking people were a delightful sensation. The fact that they were the object of discrimination and racial violence in America only added to the piquancy of their presence in Russia.

Now that dark-hued peoples are appearing in large numbers in Russia, the novelty has worn off. Unfortunately, many

Russians have never had training in coping with problems of race. They have merely been told that these problems do not exist in the Soviet Union. In the actuality of the situation they react with a primitivism little different from that encountered in other parts of the world.

And this would seem to underscore Homer Smith's major thesis: that the Soviet Union is no utopia; that we can not run away from our problems; we merely run into others which may differ from those we know but are no less serious.

The moral of Homer Smith's experience is clear. No human or social gain can be achieved without suffering and sacrifice. There are no packaged answers. In each society the road toward a better life and deeper understanding is paved with pain and struggle.

Harrison Salisbury

TABLE OF CONTENTS

AUTHOR'S PREFACE

Many of my friends and acquaintances, both white and Negro, often asked me since my long Russian Odyssey ended after World War II, why I had not written a book about Russia as seen through the eyes of an American Negro. The fact that there had already been a plethora of books about Russia, they felt, was beside the point. They also insisted that I was the only person uniquely qualified to do such a book.

To these friends and acquaintances, I replied and pleaded in extenuation, that a book by me, about Russia, would have to take the form of a memoir. A memoir, in my opinion, should never be written too quickly after an experience or event, but should be mulled over, reminisced, allowed to simmer, ripen and age in the perspective of time.

There have been other, more pressing, reasons for the delay. In my particular case, with contractual committments to time-consuming duties, there just has not been available the needed time to undertake the writing of a book. Now, during the past year, I have been fortunate enough to find the necessary time. This book therefore represents a long cherished desire to set down some of my intensive and extensive Russian experiences, observations, and impressions in book form.

The reader is forewarned that if he expects to find in these pages any deliberate axe-grinding, he will be disappointed, unless the reader wishes to be so unrealistic as to see in truth an attempt at axe-grinding. My purpose in this book is to relate faithfully and factually some of the things I saw, heard and came up against during my lengthy Russian experience.

The reader is reminded that he will find, here and there, some of my own reactions in the form of comment. Human beings always react in one way or another to external stimuli and surroundings. I am a human being. Too, I feel that it would be short-changing the reader and dishonest to myself if my personal reactions were not included in this memoir. My reactions are entirely my own. They are in nowise intended to influence the reader one way or another.

I might add, quite frankly, that I still have a certain lingering nostalgia for Russia—but for a Russia far different from the Russia that I came to know so well.

Minneapolis, Minnesota   HOMER SMITH
April, 1964

A wise man changes his mind,
A fool never.

—Spanish Proverb

CHAPTER I

Through the Window: Minneapolis to Moscow

This will be my window upon the West
—Peter the Great

WHAT HAD STARTED ME, *a twenty-two year old American Negro*, on the long road from Minneapolis to Moscow? To be free, to walk in dignity—for these precious privileges some men will go anywhere, sacrifice anything. In quest of these rights immigrants have come from all over the world to America. I yearned to stand taller than I had ever stood to breathe total freedom in great exhilarating gulps, to avoid all the hurts that were increasingly becoming the lot of men (and women) of color in the United States. The solution seemed simple to me: Russia was the only place where I could go and escape color discrimination entirely. Moscow seemed the answer.

As a student at the University of Minnesota in the School of Journalism (then called Department of Journalism), I knew that the best I could ever hope for was to work, as I had been doing since my junior year, in the post office—the safe, secure job for a Negro in the thirties. Newspapers weren't hiring Negroes in those days and though I might have gotten a job on one of the Negro papers elsewhere represented on campus, it was something less than I aspired to. I read avidly the reports of the Soviet experiment, the Five Year Plan, and the classless Society that was abuilding in Russia. The *Daily Worker* wrote glowingly that Soviet Russia was the one political state which stood for social justice for all oppressed peoples.

Who, I thought, was more oppressed than the Negro? Who else was being lynched with hideous regularity? Twenty Negroes in 1930 alone. Then in 1931 the Scottsboro Case hit the front pages. Nine Negro boys were sentenced to death, for allegedly raping two white girls who were riding the same freight train with them. One day, after some heated words in a restaurant about not getting waited on, I made my decision.

Naturally, my father and mother were aghast at the idea. My staunchly Christian mother was particularly upset and tried hard to dissuade me. "Of all places, that atheistic country," she said. "France, almost any place else, but Russia—" But I was of age, earning my own money and there was nothing they could do to stop my wanderlust. I had to see for myself.

I began getting my dollars and clothes together. Being somewhat conservative, though toying with radical ideas, I had no desire to starve in the streets of Moscow. So I sent off a letter to the Moscow Post Office, stating my qualifications, and was thrilled to receive a reply almost immediately offering me a position as consultant to the Moscow Post Office at a higher salary than I was then receiving.

The Negro Press had no correspondent in Russia and the editors of the several papers I approached were agreeable that I represent them under my pen-name of Chatwood Hall, which actually was a pen-name I had coined while a university student.

I had my first contact with Russian officialdom at the border station of Byeloostrov. The customs officials were very courteous and correct, but they examined my baggage most carefully. Upon finding several American newspapers and magazines in one valise, they requested me to leave them at the customs station, assuring me that they would be sent on later to my Moscow address. They never arrived.

White lettering on a red streamer across the station platform pronounced: "Workers of all lands, Unite!" On important days, when western trade union delegations or other sympathetic groups of pilgrims to the "Fatherland of the world's toiling masses" arrived, a brass band would unfailingly be on hand blaring out the rousing strains of the *Internationalè*. Naturally there was none for me.

Ahead of me in the distance lay magnificent and sprawling Leningrad, Russia's former Imperial City. Peter the Great had ordered its construction, naming it Saint Petersburg and referring to it as "My Paradise" and "Russia's window upon the West." It was now to be my window into Russia.

My hotel room window opened upon broad and arrow-straight Nevsky Prospect, long one of Europe's famous thoroughfares. It had been named after the feudal-military Grand Prince-Saint Alexander Nevsky, who had defeated the German Knights on the ice of nearby Lake Pskov back in the thirteenth century. And though the Bolsheviks, after the 1917 revolution, had re-named it October Twenty-fifth Street, almost seventeen years after the revolution Russians still nostalgically referred to it as Nevsky Prospect.

Although Leningrad appeared to be in a state of studied neglect, despite the fact that it bore Lenin's name, its unmistakable mellow beauty and grandeur could still be discerned. Its chief architect had been Dominico Tresini.

At the head of the street rose the slender gilded spire of the sprawling Admiralty, topped by a weathercock in the form of a ship. Two nymphs holding a globe guarded the entrance to this cavernous structure. It had been the nucleus both of the city and for Peter the Great's plans for the expansion of Russia's sea power in the Gulf of Finland and the Baltic Sea.

As I wandered about Leningrad I found stately and elaborate buildings, many of them of great beauty, facing straight, long streets and spacious, harmonious squares. The baroque of Rastrelli, the transition style of De La Mothe and Rinaldi, and the classical and Empire styles of Guarenghi and Rossi were everywhere.

I wandered through the General Staff Arch and looming before me, like a whale on some distant strand, was the dark baroque bulk of the Winter Palace. Between me and the palace, in the center of the vast square, towered Montferrand's Alexander Column, supporting on its summit an angel holding a cross.

The great palace, Rastrelli's baroque masterpiece, with its seven hundred rooms, had been turned into the Museum of the Revolution. Other great architectural gems, I soon found, also were being made to serve the Revolution.

Under the great dome of Montferrand's St. Isaac's Cathedral an anti-religious museum strove to inculcate atheism into the traditionally deeply-religious Russian people. The lovely yellow palace of Prince Yusupoff, created by the genius of Guarenghi, and in the basement of which the mystical monk Gregory Rasputin had been murdered, now housed Communist indoctrination classes.

Passing along Voznesensky Street, there loomed before me the domed Tauride Palace, which had been the seat of the Czarist Russian Duma. A bitter struggle for power between the duly constituted Provisional Government and the Bolsheviks was waged in this palace in 1917. Inside its walls the Czar's Ministers had been arrested. The first official cries of "All power to the Soviets" were first heard here, and in Room 13 was issued Soviet Ukase (Decree) No. 1, relieving soldiers of the obligation of saluting their officers. Little did I suspect that during the coming years I would see Russia and the Russian people ruled by a continuing stream of decrees.

One of my strolls about the city brought me to Smolny Institute, a former boarding school where girls from genteel Russian families were educated and raised to be ladies in the fullest sense of that word. Through the long, snow-white corridors of this classical structure, where in pre-Revolution days girls had tripped lightly to and from their classes, I now heard the thuds of the heavy boots of Communist Party functionaries. In Rooms 10 and 17, a guide explained, the 1917 *coup d'état* had been planned. In two modest rooms down another corridor, the real leaders of the Russian Revolution, Vladimir Lenin and Leon Trotsky, had lived and plotted the take over of power.

In another, Joseph Stalin had sat glumly sucking his pipe and dreaming of the day when, after the passing of these two intellectual giants, who far overshadowed him, he would grasp unchallenged power for himself and wield it with bloody brutality. His chance was to come when Lenin died in 1924; and soon afterwards he exiled Trotsky to the wilderness. Trotsky was assassinated by Jacque Mornard in Mexico City in 1940, some say at the instigation of the Kremlin.

Down the corridor from where I stood, blood was later shed in the continual intriguing and plotting that followed Stalin's ascension to power. Sergei Kirov, who was the Communist boss of Leningrad and who aspired to become Stalin's heir, was assassinated here on December 1, 1934. This assassination was used as a pretext for a paroxysm of terror—thousands of executions and the exile of tens of thousands of Russians. These excesses culminated in the great purges of 1936–38, which sent still more thousands of Russians before firing squads or to exile in the Siberian taiga, that vast swampy region of pines that begins where the tundra ends.

So despite the architectural grandeur of Leningrad, a depressive aura prevailed everywhere. Poverty and hunger

gripped Russia's former Imperial City. The people were shab-
bily dressed, obviously haggard, with tired, woebegone faces.
"Peter's Paradise" seemed to have been unkind to them both
physically and spiritually. But Leningrad, I conjectured, was
situated on the northwestern fringe of Russia, far from the
vast and fertile hinterland steppes, which at one time had
served as the breadbasket for much of Europe. Things would
be better there, I thought, and I was anxious to be on my way.

CHAPTER II

Moscow Neophyte: 1932

O Moscow . . . for a Russian heart
How much is mingled in that sound!
                    —Pushkin's *Eugene Onegin*

M Y FIRST IMPRESSIONS of Moscow were that my over-night train ride had taken me into a different country. It was as if I'd left Europe and entered Asia. Leningrad was European; Moscow was Eurasian. Indeed, Peter the Great had become so exasperated with Moscow's persistent provincialism that he had abandoned the city as Russia's capital and ordered Saint Petersburg created as the country's new Europeanized capital.

Moscow's narrow and crooked cobble-stoned streets, the profusion of onion-shaped church domes, the thoroughfares teeming with motley masses of coarse and rude people—rustic and bearded peasants shuffling along in bast sandals, seemingly aimlessly, and moving in single file with the men in front and the women following—surely this was not Europe. It struck me as being a demi-world somewhere between Europe and Asia.

I did not know a soul in this sprawling and teeming city, capital of one-sixth of the earth and seat of Soviet power, the citadel of world Communist revolution. From an expatriate Russian couple who had been my fellow passengers as we crossed the Atlantic by boat, I had learned about twenty words of Russian. They had been "going home to Socialist Mother Russia" after having lived for ten years in capitalist America. (Incidentally, I met this same couple two years later. They had one-way tickets back to America.)

My home in Moscow for the next twelve months was to be the Mininskaya Hotel, a small second-rate hostel on Vasilyevskaya Proyezd, which sloped sharply off from Red Square down to the Moscow River. The hotel stood in the shadow of the tall Gothic Spassky Gate Tower of the Kremlin. On the second day after my arrival, I decided to walk up to famous Red Square and take a look through the Spassky Gate into the Kremlin. I took a position directly across from the gate alongside the fence of bizarre Saint Basil's Cathedral, But hardly had I taken up my vantage point before a militiaman sauntered over from the gate and politely requested me to move on.

The reason, I later learned, was that top-ranking Communist personalities used this gate to enter and leave the Kremlin in their big American cars and anyone, Russian or foreigner, loitering near the gate became suspect. However, I did succeed in getting a glimpse of a chauffeur-driven car passing out the gate that day. In it was a well-dressed woman. She had on a fur stole, despite the fact that it was high summer, and I imagined she was the wife or sweetheart of one of the Kremlin VIP's.

Every night at nine o'clock I was serenaded by the melodious chimes in the Spassky Gate Tower pealing out the *Internationalè*. Often I went into flood-lit Red Square to listen closer to this rallying melody of the oppressed and exploited of the world. Knots of foreign tourists, many of them from America, were usually there listening to this "sweet music" without realizing that its written words doomed to revolutionary destruction the cherished society and institutions from which they came.

The sound of heavy explosions nearby and the rattling of the windows of my room late every night aroused my curiosity —and some concern. Was a counter-revolution in progress? I inquired of the humble, bearded hotel porter what was causing these noctural noises and tremors. Removing his visored cap and making the sign of the cross, and in a voice filled with emotion, he gave me the explanation in understandable English.

On the other side of the Kremlin, on the bank of the Moscow River, there had stood, since 1833, the massive and venerated Cathedral of the Saviour, the largest church in Moscow, built to commemorate the liberation of Moscow from Napoleon in 1812. Only recently it had been pulled down and charges of dynamite were being exploded nightly to uproot every trace even of its foundation. I was never able to learn why the dynamiting was done only at night, but I presumed it was because the passing streets were free of traffic.

My first task in Moscow was to report for work in the post office. A spacious office was assigned to me on the ground floor of the three-story graystone building which was formerly the old Czarist Post Office overlooking busy Myasnitskaya Ulitsa (Butchers' Street). My staff was to consist of three persons— Madam X, my personal interpreter; Boris Novikov, a veteran postal employee, who was to be my personal assistant; and Ludmilla Gneditch, my translator-typist. They all knew English surprisingly well.

But my office was almost bare, except for a large picture of Stalin beaming down from one of the walls, for the Cult of Personality was in full swing. I drew up a list of needed appurtenances—desks, chairs, typewriters (one with an English keyboard, the other with Russian characters), a supply of paper, ink, pencils, etc. Moscow, like far-northern cities in America, has short hot summers and long cold winters, so I included an electric fan amongst my needs.

I turned my list over to Novikov and surprisingly enough,

within one week he had obtained everything except the type-writers. These, he said, were in extremely short supply. But two weeks later I found two typewriters in my office.

"See," Novikov said pointing, "made in America—Under-vood" Russians cannot pronounce the letter "w," there being no such letter in the Russian alphabet.

Ludmilla, buxom and with straw-colored hair parted in the middle and drawn to a large bun on the back of her head, had a family name that intrigued me. I knew that it was a Gneditch who many years ago had first translated Homer's *Illiad* and *Odyssey* into Russian. When I asked her about this she admitted that she was a direct descendant of that scholarly translator.

My next move was to draw up, with Novikov, a detailed plan of operation for my forthcoming survey. This, after completion and translation from English to Russian, was submitted to the Postmaster. He took a cursory glance at it and scratched "OK"—all the English he knew—on the bottom margin of each page.

Together with Novikov, I then began examining what already had convinced me was a bureaucratic, red-tape-ridden postal service. I found duplication of effort, lost motion, unnecessary paper work, overstaffing and downright inefficiency on all sides. We roamed the post office, as I made detailed and voluminous notes. What I saw at this early stage convinced me of the simplicity and efficiency of the U. S. Postal Service.

During all these preliminary activities, I made it plain to all postal officials that I was operating wholly objectively and would state my findings impartially in my final report. Some officials gave excellent cooperation; others proved uncooperative. But I asserted my authority and pushed ahead without fear or favor.

Through Novikov, I learned that there was widespread ri-fling of money from letters and of food from parcels. This, of course, I attributed to the scandalously low salaries and the severe food shortages. But I decided that this was outside my frame of reference, and when I told Novikov that it was a matter for the Postal Inspectors, he remarked, "But most of the inspectors are in cahoots with the thieves!"

There was one secluded section of the cavernous post office that I found was out of bounds for me. I asked Novikov why.

"That section is the Secret Department," Novikov explained. "That's all I know. I have no knowledge of what goes on in there. All I know is that only trusted Party members are permitted to enter it. I advise you to leave that section alone."

This caused me to assume that this was top-secret territory where letters to Russians from abroad and letters from Russians to foreign countries were "processed"—that is, censored. I took Novikov's advice and did not try to make a survey of that sensitive area. And I recalled that the Chief of the Third Department (Secret Police), under Nicholas I, Count A. K. Benckendorf, once remarked back in the early nineteenth century: "One of the best resources the secret police have is to intercept correspondence; it is always effective."

At this time it was also made clear to me that my scope of operations was not to be limited to Moscow, nor would I be tied down to my desk in the ordinary nine-to-five routine. Field trips to study the operational problems of other Soviet post offices were likely to be frequent and this I welcomed, for I had a vast curiosity about the rest of the country. And even then I was hoping to get back into journalism, which had been my main interest in college. So the more I traveled, I reasoned, the more I would have to write about eventually, if ever I got back to writing again.

The job, however, proved to be less pleasant and rewarding than outward appearances had indicated, even though it was challenging. The post office was in a mess, as I surmised, all bogged down in a mass of paperwork. Inefficiency and plain laziness were rampant; there appeared to be more people sitting

at tables and desks and filling in forms and rustling through
some kinds of paper work than were actually handling the
mails. Postal employees were underpaid and underfed; red tape
and bureaucracy filled the place like a fog. My job was to advise how matters might be improved so that the mails would
move smoothly and quickly, as in American post offices.

The first few months I spent making inspections of the central post office and the city's branch postal stations. I even
explored Russian railway mail cars. Then I got busy preparing
my preliminary recommendations, assisted by my faithful Russian woman interpreter, translator and typist.

These were highly critical of red tape, bureaucracy, paper
work, low salaries, and general inefficiency. I offered positive
and detailed methods for removing most of the roadblocks to
simplification and efficiency, at least in the Moscow area. The
postmaster received these initial recommendations eagerly and
with expressions of appreciation, and promised that as many
of my suggestions as possible would be "put into life."

Meanwhile, I spent my free time learning the extremely
difficult Russian language and becoming better acclimated to
my new environment. Of my newly acquired friends, the Russian lady who acted as my tutor provided most of my introduc-
tions to Moscow mores and my initiation into the vagaries of
Soviet political life.

Madame Sonya, though that was not her name, was the
daughter of a former Czarist general and landowner. She
had an excellent command of languages, speaking fluent English, German, French and Italian. Her education had been obtained at the Smolny Institute in Leningrad and at finishing
schools in Vienna and Geneva. Twice a week I went to her for
my Russian lesson.

She lived with her aged mother and young son in two small
rooms on the second floor of a dilapidated pre-Revolution
building just off Arbat Square. Like many of the old Russian
aristocracy, they were gracious and genteel people. The mother

insisted on calling me her grandson and demanded that I call her grandmother. The young boy immediately nicknamed me "Gospodin (Mr.) Pushkin," perhaps because like that illustrious poet I was dark-skinned and had frizzy hair.

During my visits I noticed on the walls a profusion of photographs and pictures of Madame's family during the days before the Revolution. There were interior and exterior views of their lovely and spacious mansion in Saint Petersburg; family scenes of outings and picnics at their summer home on the shore of the Gulf of Finland; pictures of Madame's father in the uniform of a Czarist General; and family photographs taken at famous European spas. Then one day I noticed that all the pictures had disappeared from the walls. I tactfully asked what had become of them. Covering her eyes with her hands and sobbing gently, she told me why the cherished photos had been removed. As she talked, I recalled that Robert Burns had said that man's inhumanity to man makes countless thousands mourn.

It seemed that the house manager, a Communist Party member, had made an inspection tour of the building a few days before and had devoted himself to a particularly close study of the photographs on the wall. He had asked several provocative questions, then slammed the door as he left. Later the same day when Madame went to his office for her monthly ration card, he had refused to give it to her, remarking sarcastically that food was too scarce for feeding her kind.

I was infuriated. After all, this gentlewoman was no more responsible for her birth in an aristocratic family than I had been for mine in a Negro family. Furthermore, her family had been dispossessed by the Bolsheviks without compensation, and now with their meager rations cut off, faced starvation.

Determined that these kind and proud people should not go hungry, I made two proposals. One was that instead of paying rubles for my Russian lessons, since without a ration card the rubles would have been useless anyway, I be permitted to bring food from the *Torgsin* shops, which were well stocked with food of all kinds and sold only to foreigners for foreign currency. The second proposal was that on my "study" days I take my meals at her house with grandmother preparing the food that I brought. They were overjoyed at this arrangement.

One day later in the week, as I was leaving the building, the house manager sidled up to me.

"*Tovarish,* could you bring *me* a bottle of Zubrovka from *Torgsin?*"

"Nyet! Nyet! Nyet!" I shouted at him.

However, afterward I had second thoughts and relented. The next day I eased him a bottle of this most powerful and potent Russian liquor. This I did not out of any kindly feeling toward him, but merely hoping that by "cooperating" with him I might thereby lessen the hardships of my friends upstairs. He invited me into his office to have a swig with him; and later my friends said that he had even begun speaking or bowing to them as they went out of the building, something he had never done before.

While sitting one day by a window talking with grandmother, I heard the surging strains of a brass band coming down Arbat Street. The marchers were loudly singing the *Internationalè.* Grandmother got up, closed the window, and snatched the blinds shut.

"I don't want to see or hear that misguided rabble," she remarked angrily. She had never reconciled herself to the Soviet regime, and until her death, in 1937, she remained an unyielding and proud Russian aristocrat.

One day I arrived and found an extremely beautiful blonde young woman at Madame Sonya's house. There was no mistaking that she, too, was well-bred and from a genteel family. Next day, Madame Sonya said, "That *baryshnaya* (young lady) likes you very much."

Upon assuring Madame Sonya that I was amenable, she

airily answered, "No! No! She can't have an *affaire d'amour* with you; she belongs to a very big man in the Kremlin."

I found this incident quite revealing. Outwardly, the Communist ruling class was expressing vociferous and bitter hatred of the old Russian bourgeoisie, of which this lovely woman was a member. But apparently Marxist ideology and the class struggle were not to be allowed to interfere with amorous avocations, for I soon learned that most Communist philanderers were not letting their scruples interfere with their attempts to inveigle attractive, genteel women of the former upper class into clandestine affairs.

Madame Sonya's son occasionally made remarks about his father, but his mother always told him to "Hush, Hush." I never saw the boy's father, nor did Madame ever mention him. Then one Sunday, six months after my lessons began, I arrived and found him at home. He was a dark-haired, brown-eyed Russian, obviously an intellectual, about forty-five years old. Also of an aristocratic pre-Revolution family, he too spoke English, German and French.

By profession, he was a hydraulic engineer, but he said nothing about the reasons for his absence or where he had been. I tactfully did not press him, for I had learned earlier from one of Madame Sonya's friends that he had been arrested two years earlier and sent to work on the White Sea-Baltic Canal, which was then under construction. I was told that he had committed no crime, but apparently his engineering skill was needed and the end, in Soviet eyes, always justified the means. Evidently he had produced satisfactorily and was now being given a month's leave to visit his family.

Forced labor was one of the main factors in the development of the Soviet economy. It guaranteed an adequate labor force for such gigantic construction projects as the Baltic Sea-White Sea Canal, which had been assigned to the OGPU (The Unified State Political Police) in November 1931, and was completed in June, 1933. The canal was 141.05 miles long, with

19 locks, 15 dams and 32 subsidiary canals. Of the three hundred thousand workers used on the canal, seventy-two thousand were released as "rehabilitated" upon its completion. I never found out whether Madame's husband was finally released or whether his skills were needed on the Moscow-Volga Canal, which was constructed between 1933 and 1937.

I had arrived in Moscow without any preconceived ideas or convictions, though admittedly I had a tremendous amount of sympathy for what I felt the country was trying to do. My early Moscow observations had made it obvious that there were food shortages in the city, but I theorized that perhaps food supplies for the still large remnants of the former bourgeois class were being skimped in order that more food could be available for the proletarian majority. My mind was still open, but it was not to remain that way for long.

CHAPTER III

Machines Instead of Food

Technical skills and machines will decide everything.
—Second Five Year Plan slogan

Poverty was everywhere around me. In my walks about the city I found long lines of hungry men and women standing at grocery and butcher shops in the hope of getting something to eat. They began queuing up at daybreak, which was three o'clock in the morning during the summer. Most of them left, often several hours later, with only hunks of black bread and a few ounces of potatoes and sausage. Sugar and butter were rarely available. Ham, eggs and cheese were also in short supply—except in the *Torgsin* shops, which were reserved for foreigners.

Food was also scarce in my second-class hotel, which was not reserved for foreign tourists. And what there was was so insipid that I began taking my breakfast and supper in one of the Intourist (foreign tourist) hotels or in the *Torgsin* cafe on the corner of Petrovka Street and Kuxnetsky Most. These places were, of course, of no use to Russians because they accepted only valuta (foreign currency), which it was illegal for them to possess. The menus were bountiful in the midst of hunger all around me and I never ceased having a guilty feeling as I came out with my well-filled stomach.

The most popular and sought after persons in Moscow were members of the sizable foreign community, consisting mainly of Americans, Germans and English. It was reasoned by the Russians, and rightly, that these foreigners would possess foreign currency and/or passes to *Insab,* a special well-stocked food shop to which only foreigners employed by the Soviet Government had access.

As a consequence, making the acquaintance of an *inostranyet* (a foreigner) was the ambition of many Russians. Some of these acquaintances developed into deep and lasting friendships; others proved to be merely temporary expediency on the part of hungry Russians.

Communist theoreticians have always claimed that an inevitable outcome of the capitalist economic system is prostitution. Not being a political theorist or a sociologist, I don't feel qualified to argue for or against this claim, but as an on-the-spot observer, I can say that though I did not observe any organized prostitution in Moscow, as one finds in many European cities, I did see a great deal of what I can only call avocational prostitution.

Even with full employment, and in some areas even a severe shortage of labor, a foreigner with a bar of chocolate and a carton of cigarettes could create intimate friendships with some Russian women. Most of them were working in factories, or offices, on night or day shifts, and used their off-hours to engage in this avocational and sub-rosa form of prostitution. Almost without exception they preferred foreigners and food rather than money, as the ordinary Russian male had neither.

One lovely employed though hungry girl named Tamara engaged in this sub-rosa prostitution with a married foreign diplomat whose wife had not yet joined him. Tamara even moved into his quarters. Her sojourn in comfortable and spacious surroundings was rudely interrupted when the diplomat

thousands of peasants to join the collectives, farming was still being carried on. Over wide stretches of the fertile Russian steppe large amounts of foodstuffs were being produced. How then explain the paradox of food being produced and people starving. The answer was to be found in the basic needs of the Five Year Plan, the first one just ending, the second just beginning. Stalin's unwritten motto was simply: "Machines instead of Food." Consequently enormous amounts of food were being exported in exchange for western machinery and services to build the foundation for Russia's future industrialization. People were expendable. Five Year Plans were not.

CHAPTER IV

The Black and White
Film Fiasco

The Soviet Union is the Fatherland of the toilers and oppressed of the world. —Communist slogan

THE ISSUE OF RACE in the United States had long intrigued the Russian propaganda chiefs, and then, as now, they quickly seized upon every racial incident in America, no matter how minor, to make grist for the Communist propaganda mill.

That many non-Communist Americans fell prey to the propaganda was only indicative of the naïveté and innocence of the Americans. The case of the *Black and White* film production is an example.

Early in 1932 a decision was reached in Moscow to dramatize the American race problem. The instrument for the dramatization was to be a motion picture which would be exhibited around the world, especially in the colored countries of Asia and Africa, as "documentary" proof of the manner in which capitalist America discriminated against and oppressed its colored citizens.

At an early stage in the preparations, the Russians had intended using a Russian cast, blackening their faces with burnt cork and putting kinky wigs on their heads. But this idea was soon dropped, it being decided that such ersatz Negroes would prove neither convincing nor capable of providing the proper emotional intensity.

It was then agreed that real Negroes should be brought from America. In the United States a sponsoring committee was formed primarily of very well thought of citizens, both Negro and white. Among the sponsors were Bessye Bearden, George S. Counts, Malcolm Cowley, Rose McLendon, John B. Hammond, Jr., and Will Vodery. The film's purpose, according to the sponsors, was to present a "realistic and historical picture of the Negro race in the United States which the producers hoped would reveal the Negro to the (Russian) workers and knit a closer cultural bond between the peoples of the two countries."

The motion picture was to be filmed in English and titled *Black and White*, the locale being Birmingham, Alabama. Its heroes and heroines were to be Negro laborers. The men were stokers in the steel mills, the women, domestics in rich white homes. The leading role, a progressive labor organizer, was to be played by a white man, who wanted Negroes and whites to be organized into one labor union, a forerunner of the CIO. And villians, of course, were the steel mill bosses and the absentee landlords from the North, who kept the workers, both white and black, out of the union and fighting each other.

In response to an invitation from the Meschrabpom Film Corporation of Moscow, an eager band of young Negroes volunteered. One has only to remember that even today the Negro actor can find scant work in Hollywood, to understand the alacrity with which actors and writers jumped at the chance to travel abroad at someone else's expense and to work in a media that was all but closed to them at home.

They came from such distances as California, Minnesota, Virginia, New England and even Montego Bay, Jamaica. Langston Hughes traveled by car, from the Pacific to the Atlantic Coast, in order not to miss the boat. Wayland Rudd, who had worked in "Porgy"; Taylor Gordon, writer and concert singer; Loren Miller, now a prominent Los Angeles attorney; Ted R. Poston, New York newsman; and Henry Lee Moon, prominent publicist and author, were all amongst the twenty-two passengers as the North Bremen liner *Europa* sailed past the Statue of Liberty on June 14, 1932, bound for the fatherland of the world's oppressed.

In mid-ocean the voyagers (tourist class) unexpectedly met and discussed their adventure with Dr. Ralph Bunche and Dr. Alain Locke (first class passengers) on their way to Paris. These two distinguished intellectuals, both Howard University professors, showed a keen interest in the project and wished their fellow countrymen well.

After six uneventful days on the *Europa,* the group reached Bremerhaven. The boat train rushed them to Berlin within a few hours and it was here that they met their first snag. Unfortunately, it was not to be the last. To the traveler, the visa is the open sesame, the welcome mat. Without it you are an unwelcome nonentity, which was exactly the situation they faced upon arrival in Berlin. No Russian visas awaited them. Visas could not be obtained in New York because there were then no diplomatic relations between the United States and Russia. And the Russian Consul in Berlin had never even heard of the group, or so he said.

It had been expected that the Berlin representative of the Moscow film studio had arranged for visas and would meet them with contracts ready for signing. None of these arrangements had been made, and twenty-two Negro Americans found themselves in Berlin without visas, without contracts and with fast-dwindling pocket money.

After many heated exchanges on the telephone to Moscow, visas were finally issued and the group set off again for Russia, this time on board a Finnish ship across the Baltic Sea, then by rail through Finland across northern Russia to Moscow.

When finally they arrived at Moscow's Nikolayevsky Railway Station, about the only thing missing was a brass band. The handful of Negroes then living in Moscow had been rounded up to join the welcoming party. There, smiling from ear to ear, was old and wizened Emma, the Mammy of Moscow, who had lived in Russia for thirty years. Behind her could be seen two very dark and very Negroid welcomers, both named Bob, one Ross, the other Robinson. Lovett Forte-Whiteman, a member of the Russian team that had written the scenario was there, as was I. As the newcomers alighted from the train, Emma crowed, "Lord a'mighty, my people don' arrived." Of course, many official Russians were there, all smiles and glad hands to greet what they expected to be typical American representatives of the toiling black masses.

The morning after their arrival the Negroes were brought together at the Meschrabpom Film Studio to meet the director, Karl Younghans, and his assistants. There were raised eyebrows and puzzled expressions and whispered asides among the Russians. These were the toiling masses of American Negroes?

There before the astonished Russians stood twenty-two men and women ranging in color from dark brown to high yellow. "We needed genuine Negroes and they sent us a bunch of metisi (mixed bloods)," one disturbed Russian remarked in an undertone. Another puzzled official shook his head after shaking hands with several members of the group. "Their hands, so soft, they don't feel like workers hands."

The truth of the matter was that none of the group came within the category of worker. Most of them were college trained and belonged to what could be called the intellectual or white collar class. It is doubtful whether any of them had ever seen a steel mill in operation, much less worked in one. There most certainly were no callous-handed sharecroppers, stevedores or truck drivers—the types the Russians had expected—among them. Furthermore, most of them had never even experienced the ruder and cruder forms of Jim Crow, having lived North of the Mason-Dixon line.

The group was quartered at the Grand Hotel. Do not be misled, it might have been grand during the time of the Czars and even now was one of the better hotels, but it still left much to be desired. With the acute food shortage then prevailing in Russia, there was great difficulty in catering to American appetites. The Grand Hotel dining room had no menu; guests sat down and were served whatever was available. Day after day this consisted of weak Russian borsch, some Irish potatoes, cabbage and black bread. No pork chops, no chicken, no ham and eggs, no butter. It didn't take long for the quiet grumbling to reach overwhelmingly vocal proportions. Something had to be done and quickly, or the Negroes might have staged a strike, in spite of the fact that strikes were banned in Russia.

Consequently, a couple of wheezy old trucks were rounded up and dispatched into the nearby countryside to forage for food. The trucks returned, loaded with chickens, eggs, vegetables and meat . . . bought from farmers, who despite collectivization and the shortage of food in the state shops, were stashing away provisions for such lucrative private trading.

These foraged provisions were then turned over to the hotel's kitchen with strict orders that they were to be prepared and served only to the Negro tovarischi. With full stomachs, ample supplies of vodka, and with the keys to the city, the Negro members of the *Black and White* film company settled down to enjoy themselves.

Meanwhile, Langston Hughes, whose job it was to give advice on the script, was completely bogged down. The scenario had been prepared without benefit of American advice. It is true that Lovett Forte-Whiteman worked on the project, but he was a Negro intellectual and so steeped in party dogma that he had completely lost touch with America. Russian scenario writers had never been closer than six thousand miles to the United States and had used their imaginations much too freely. The fact that they were so completely taken aback by the wide range of skin colors amongst the American cast was an example of their unfamiliarity with American reality, and this during the period when Stanislavsky and others were campaigning for realism in the theater!

After weeks of wrangling with the Russians over a script that just did not fit the reality of Negro-white relations in the United States, Langston finally convinced the producers that the scenario was beyond any revision or rewriting. It had to be scrapped and, with Langston's help, an entirely new script was to be prepared.

This, of course, would take time, but the Russians seemed so sincerely determined in their efforts to make the film that they were ready to start afresh.

What with plenty of time on their hands, enough rubles to choke a horse, any expression of racial prejudice or color discrimination taboo, things had never been so good for the Negro tovarischi. A member of the company from Virginia found a fiancée and was soon married. The studio's lovely Russian leading lady fell desperately in love with a member of the group from Minnesota. And while boating on the Moscow River, under the crenelated walls of the Kremlin, one of the more ardent members of the group and his Russian girl friend become so engrossed with each other that they failed to notice that their leaky skiff was sinking. Friendly Russians dragged them out of the water.

One evening, after I had finished work at the post office, Langston and I had a date to meet at my hotel. I had asked Ala, the Russian girl that I had been dating, to bring along one of her friends for Langston. It was a lovely summer night, such as you find only near the Arctic Circle, a sort of prolonged twilight, and we had planned to spend the evening at the pleasant and popular Aquarium Summer Garden.

The two girls arrived on schedule and then trouble began.

Ala, my girl, liked Langston and her friend Vera, it appeared, had taken a fancy to me. This would have been all right, but Langston and I preferred it as we had originally planned. When I tried to explain this to the girls they started a loud argument between themselves.

Not wanting to have the floor clerk complain about the noise, I asked the girls to wait downstairs outside the hotel entrance. When Langston and I came down, they were busily engaged in pulling each other's hair in a brawl that would have done justice to 125th Street and 7th Avenue. Several passing Russian pedestrians muttered, "Ne Kulturnie" (It's not cultured).

Langston shook his head in wonderment. "Man, I've seen us fighting over white women, but this is the first time I've seen white women fighting over us."

Langston and I intervened and we proceeded to the Aquarium Summer Garden for an evening of refreshment and "kulturna."

Briefly, the *Black and White* crew were having a ball and really shaking up old Muscovy. They had taken to cavorting nude among the nude Russians without incident in the Moscow River near the Park of Culture and Rest. They were demonstrating nightly Harlem's terpsichorean art with charming Russian girls in the ballroom of the ritzy Metropole Hotel, and with such finesse and gusto as the establishment had never seen before, or perhaps since. One lanky New Yorker, Ted Poston, now a feature writer on the *New York Post,* was long afterwards remembered as Daddy Long Legs, because of his dancing prowess.

The attractive women of the group were not pining either. Russian men are known to have a deep preference for dark-skinned women. Indeed, Constantine Oumansky, at that time chief of the Press Division of the Foreign Affairs Commissiariat, was on the verge of becoming mentally unbalanced in his ardor for the smiles and favors of chic, bob-haired, peach-colored Mildred Jones of New York. Most of the girls from the cast were dated for days in advance.

But the days of joy in this Russian "Hollywood" were numbered. Secret, backroom power politics was soon to wreck the new script, the director's career and the histrionic aspirations of twenty-two would-be film stars.

As I mentioned earlier, Russia and the United States had no diplomatic relations at this time. There was some trade between the two countries, but Stalin was eager to boost this manyfold in order to assure the success of his second Five Year Plan, which was then just beginning.

Diplomatic recognition by the United States would be the open sesame for obtaining large American credits. Great quantities of American machinery could be imported and American engineering and technical personnel would come to build new factories to speed up Russia's industrialization. One would have been naïve indeed to expect Stalin to risk his promising chances of obtaining diplomatic recognition from Washington for the short-range propaganda success of mounting a film exposing America's racial problem.

Soon feelers were being put out by both sides for the resumption of normal diplomatic relations. With western industry and markets wallowing in the sloughs of the prevailing economic depression, American bankers and industrialists were more than eager to offer their services and products to the unlimited Russian market. Moscow gold carried no stigma for them.

On November 16, 1933, President Franklin Delano Roosevelt extended American diplomatic recognition to Russia. But this recognition carried a stipulation demanding that the Kremlin "refrain from propaganda against the policies or social order of the United States." And *Black and White* was obviously one of those propaganda activities.

With dramatic suddenness, word came down from above, without explanation, that the making of *Black and White* must immediately be stopped. The film director found himself in a quandary. How could he explain to the American Negro cast as painlessly as possible that the project had been canceled? He was well aware that if he passed on the bad news to them in Moscow there would inevitably be angry outcries that might be heard all over the city.

Keeping the secret well guarded, it was decided to get the cast out of town, ostensibly on a free deluxe tour through southern Russia and a long cruise on the Black Sea along the coast of the Caucasus. The studio officials felt it would be the better part of wisdom to have the group as far away from Moscow as possible before dropping their bombshell.

When the group returned to Odessa from their cruise, refreshed and in high spirits from the sea air and the beauty of the distant snow-capped Caucasus mountains, an emissary arrived from Moscow and found them lolling in the luxurious comforts of the exquisite Londres Hotel.

When he announced that the film could not be made because of "technical difficulties," moans and groans could be heard throughout the hotel's corridors. The emissary hinted, as another ruse to keep the anguished Negroes from returning to Moscow, that the group could all leave for home directly from Odessa, "without the discomfort of having to travel the long distance back to Moscow."

But this did not work, for the cast loudly demanded tickets immediately on the fastest train to Moscow so they could tell their "betrayers" face-to-face what they thought of them.

It was no Grand Hotel in Moscow this time. They were packed into the lower second-class Minimskaya Hotel just off Red Square, where I had stayed my first weeks in Moscow. It was more of a flophouse than a hotel, and only added more heat to the pent-up anger of the group.

With tempers on edge, some of the group wanted to proceed immediately to the Kremlin to protest directly to Stalin.

Others suggested marching into the Comintern to make their plaints heard by all the leaders of the world revolution. It apparently never occurred to them that they would have been shot had they tried to enter those secret and heavily-guarded bastions of Communism.

Their fury was partly spent in inter-group bickerings and some solace was no doubt found in heavy draughts of vodka. But most of the emotion was directed at the studio director, whose office was turned into near pandemonium when his cast came face-to-face with him. He was roundly denounced as an "opportunist," "Judas," "lackey of American racists," and a "betrayer who had sold out the Negro race."

But all of these tirades were undeserved and unjustified, for the director himself was as much the victim of high power politics as any of them. He took the sharp denunciations calmly, assuring the group that they were all welcome to remain in Russia, though those who wanted to return to America would be guaranteed first-class transportation. Wayland Rudd and Lloyd Patterson were the only two who decided to stay on permanently. The others ultimately returned to the U. S. My friend, Langston Hughes, picked the long way round and returned to the U. S. via China.

Aside from the emotional heat generated in this disappointed circle, the summer climate in Moscow brings uncomfortably high temperatures. To escape this heat, I sought temporary quarters in a Moscow suburb.

I found therein a small room which I rented from a family in a district known as Marina Roscha. The house, well built of hewn logs, and with gingerbread woodwork around the windows, doors and gate, was set back in a yard full of flowers and shrubbery. There was something idyllic about the premises.

Marina Roscha appeared to be an excellent, quiet place to read, write and relax. About a twenty-minute walk beyond its outskirts stood the most aesthetically pleasing structure in the whole neighborhood—the lovely eighteenth century palace of Count Sheremetyev, with the paths through the vast park surrounding it lined with classical sculptured figures.

Two weeks after I moved in, my summer hosts, a middle-aged factory worker and his wife, went away to spend a three weeks' vacation with relatives in a small town about sixty miles away. They insisted that I accompany them; I readily agreed, but with the proviso that I would stay only one week. Upon leaving we carefully locked the house, and I even put a stout American padlock on the door of my own room.

Upon returning to Marina Roscha a week later, I found the lock on the outer door and the padlock on my own room door in perfect order. But entering my room, I found that two suits of clothes that had been hanging on a nail on the wall and a pair of pants that had been laid across the foot of the bed were missing. My Baby Ben alarm clock was not on the table in front of the window. My portable typewriter was lying on its side on the floor.

Examination of the window clearly showed that it had not been jimmied open. It had not been burglary, for the house had not been broken into. How, then, had the theft been committed?

There could be but one explanation. Windows on all Russian houses have at the top, for ventilation purposes, a small hinged aperture known as a fortochka. And I recalled that I had left this unlatched. The thief obviously had used a pole with a hook or grapple on it to commit the theft. My typewriter, evidently, had proved too difficult to "fish" out.

Before my suburbanite tenure ended I was to discover that Marina Roscha was a slum, the like of which I had seen nowhere in America. The one-and two-story houses were all built of logs and were pre-Revolution structures. They were jammed with people. There was no running water, which had to be obtained from the public pumps on street corners. Only dugout privies, either attached to the sides of houses or in backyards, were available. And after the rains the streets became a quagmire.

Many nights were an olfactory horror. These were the nights when the scavengers cleaned out the privies, using buckets on ropes and transferring the excrement into horse-drawn tank-wagons. When these "sanitary" activities were in progress, the offensive stench caused residents even to close their fortochkas.

Marina Roscha, even before the Revolution, I was to learn, had been the haunt of burglars, thieves, pickpockets and other shady characters. Soviet society had not yet reformed it nor caused it to outlive its disreputable past. Yet, some honest and respectable people had to live in Marina Roscha, housing being unavailable in congested Moscow. For the time being I was one of them, but I was not sorry to move back into Moscow again, which I did as fast as I could find myself a room.

CHAPTER V

Emma: Mammy of Moscow

. . . I'd walk a million miles for one of your smiles, my Mammy.
—from American song, *Mammy*.

Any americans, colored or white, who spent any time in Moscow were sooner or later sure to meet Emma. If they did not look up Emma, Emma was sure to come looking for them.

Emma told me she had been born "down South" and had reached Russia "a long time ago," though she never explained how. There was still some physical evidence, despite her wrinkled face, graying hair and sixty odd years, that in her younger days Emma had been a very comely brown-skinned woman. Indeed, a pre-Revolution Russian nobleman, with a sharp eye for such physical attributes, had installed her, it was rumored, in a comfortable mansion.

Before the Bolsheviks took over in 1917, Emma had lived the good life in her spacious home, with three Russian servants at her beck and call.

"Now them Reds got me holed up in one room," Emma bemoaned. "They took away my big house and moved ten Russian families into it."

Langston Hughes recalls Emma telling him, "I'm like a cat with nine lives, honey. I always lands on my feet . . . been doing it all my life wherever I been. These Bolsheviks ain't gonna kill me."

Emma's one room was in an old building near three railway stations. When I asked her why she remained living in this smoky, smelly, noisy area, she answered, "Man, you ain't seen no rooms for rent signs in Moscow, have you?"

But, she added, she had another very important reason also for living where she did. "If anything busts loose against them Bolshies, I'm gonna highball out'a here on the first and fastest train out of one of them stations for anywhere on down the line."

Having been well-to-do before the Revolution, Emma was now listed in the category of the declassé bourgeoisie. She expressed undisguised bitterness over her present lot, and her criticism of prevailing conditions and the Soviet regime was sharp and openly expressed. She even praised old Czarist times, and if made by a Russian, her remarks would have landed him in Siberia.

Even in the presence of Russians—and everybody seemed to know her—I heard Emma boast about how she would "just love" to be Stalin's cook and how she'd put enough poison in his first meal to kill a mule. But the authorities never laid a hand on Emma, and I suspect that her Russian friends got a great deal of vicarious pleasure out of listening to Emma's open lambasting of the Soviet regime, a thing they themselves feared to do.

Emma had lived so long in Moscow that she spoke English haltingly and with a Russian accent. Though her use of English may have been affected, she had lost none of her culinary skill and this made Emma very popular with the American colony. With her Lithuanian servant, she had improvised a kitchen in the common corridor of the building where she lived, and the two of them were often busy with their pots and pans cooking up hash, pork and beans, beef stew, cabbage and ham hocks, fried chicken, and corn bread and muffins. The appetizing odors that wafted through the length and breadth of that old building made many Russian mouths water, for though the tenants were not acquainted with her "exotic" fare, they did know what smelled good. And Emma's cooking sure smelled good. Her clientele was strictly American, however, because her Russian neighbors had no money with which to supply the ingredients.

"Just supply me the rubles, I'll find the stuff." Emma would say to any American friends wanting some back-home cooking. Just how Emma managed to obtain the necessary food-stuffs in food-scarce Moscow nobody ever knew, or cared. If the needed ingredients could not be secured with rubles, the Americans would always hand her a few dollars so she could buy what was needed in one of the *Torgsin* shops. And Emma's bulging bag of supplies always contained a few bottles of vodka which to Emma was "Russian corn whisky."

The long years of Russian exposure had failed to erase much that was deeply-grained American in Emma, and she was frequently overcome with nostalgia. Emma's contacts were wide and varied, and she numbered many diplomatic officials among her intimate friends. As she grew older and more feeble and her desire to return home became stronger, they helped to arrange for her return to the States. When this happened the American colony in Moscow lost an irreplaceable and beloved character.

American Negroes in Russia fell into two groups, those like myself who had come since the Revolution, and those who, like Emma, had arrived in the days of the Czars. Another of these pre-Revolution Negroes was Coretta Arli-Titz, but if Emma was the Mammy of Moscow, highly urbane and sophisticated Coretta Arli-Titz was just the opposite.

She had graduated from both the Leningrad and Moscow Conservatories of Music and her present husband, a Russian named Arli-Titz, had been a noted professor of the piano at both conservatories. Coretta was still one of the most popular concert singers in Moscow and could perform fluently in four languages.

She, too, had had a wealthy, noble male "angel" in those affluent days before the Bolsheviks murdered the last of the Romanov Czars and toppled the old order. But while Emma would always refer to her former patron as having been a Grand Duke, Coretta was satisfied to refer to hers as having been a "mere" Duke. Coretta's former Duke, I learned from one of her old friends, was now driving a taxicab in Paris.

Unlike Emma, Coretta was more talkative about her past than Emma ever was. Her first public singing had been done in a Harlem church prior to World War I. There, a well-to-do visiting German woman, captivated by her promising voice, had taken her to Berlin when she was eighteen years old. From Germany she had traveled to Saint Petersburg, now Leningrad, where her ducal "angel's" influence had come to her aid.

When I first visited Coretta, she and her husband, a courtly and cultured gentleman of the old school of Russian intellectuals, were living in two small, dingy rooms in the western section of Moscow near Kropotkinskaya Square. A huge, aging grand piano occupied one-third of one room and the Russian servant girl occupied most of the other, which served as kitchen and dining room.

Although I considered these cramped quarters wholly inadequate for two persons of such high musical abilities, they were fortunate in having them—most Russian families were living in only one.

When Marian Anderson came to Moscow on one of her Russian concert tours in the mid-thirties, Coretta felt dutybound to invite the famous contralto to her home, despite an inner feeling that the visit might prove embarrassing.

A decrepit wooden gate hung lopsided at the entrance to the dirty and cobble-stoned courtyard and dark, narrow, worn stone stairs led to the dingy third-floor quarters. But Coretta, apparently outwardly unperturbed, got through her embarrassing ordeal. Besides, Marian Anderson was far too much of a lady to show that she noticed anything unusual about the cramped quarters of this foremost diva in Russia.

Unlike Emma, Coretta Arli-Titz appeared resigned to the Soviet regime, despite the fact that it had robbed her of her former "good life."

Of the two, I think, I found much more congeniality in Emma. The last time I remember seeing her was after I moved to Marina Roscha, the suburb north of Moscow.

One day, as I was strolling through the Sheremetyev Palace park, there sitting on a bench reading in the shade of an ancient oak tree beneath a white marble statue of Pan piping his flute, was old Emma.

I sat down beside the old woman, who appeared to be lost in thoughts of times past. Sitting in the shadows of the lovely rococo Sheremetyev Palace, I suspected, she was lost in nostalgia of the "good old days" when she was a "grand dame" and danced as a guest under the sparkling cut glass chandeliers in the white marble halls of that magnificent structure.

"What are you doing away out here?" I asked.

"Looking for you. Somebody told me you were living in Marina Roscha, but I didn't know your address. I just had a hunch you might be coming along."

"Are you reading an interesting book?" I asked.

"Oh, yeah, it's a new Russian edition of *Uncle Tom's Cabin*," Emma answered. "And do you know, them Bolshies done weaved in a lot of dialectical materialism. They done made a revolutionary out of Uncle Tom!"

Emma remarked that I was looking rather thin, then added: "Come up and see me some time. I'll stir up something that will fill your belly and put some meat on your bones."

I offered to walk to the bus stop with her. Pressing twenty rubles into her hand, I told her I would be hungry tomorrow.

As the bus moved away, she yelled through the open window, "Man, I'll have them pots boiling at twelve o'clock tomorrow. Come with your belly empty."

But something intervened the next day and I couldn't keep our appointment. Shortly after this, and before I had a chance to see her again, she returned to America.

CHAPTER VI

Bear Interlude

Pour couper court
—French Proverb

AMONG MY EARLY ACQUAINTANCES were several persons in the theatrical worlds of the Kamerny, Meyerhold, Art, Gypsy, Vakhtagov and Jewish theaters. Comparatively better paid and housed, they were the Bohemians of Moscow. They were deeply dedicated to their work and most of them told me confidentially that they had utter contempt for politics. They only attended under pressure the endless "production" and "political indoctrination" meetings called by the artistically-ignorant secretaries of the Communist Party cells attached to their theaters.

Some of my theatrical friends spoke of protracted bickering over "ideology" and "realism" and "formalism" between ignorant Party secretaries and expert, veteran theater directors. These "ideological" squabbles between political functionaries and the better directors inevitably resulted directly in the downfall and subsequent liquidation of such theatrical geniuses as Tairov and Meyerhold.

One of my best and most sincere friends, the brilliant actor

and founder of the Moscow Yiddish Theater, Schlomo Mikoels, was similarly "liquidated." Mikoels was one of the ugliest
men I have even seen—big mouth, full lips with the bottom
one hanging down, and wild-looking bushy, frizzled hair. But
he was a great impresario and actor. He worked hard building
the Moscow Yiddish Theater into one of Russia's best. He was
a supporter of the Communist regime, and probably a member
of the Party, for he never showed any disdain over Communist dictatorship. When was he liquidated? I wouldn't know
. . . Thousands of persons were liquidated without court
trials—they merely disappeared and it was only later that one
learned of their fate. My assumption is that he fell into dis-
favor for emphasizing the old heroes of the Jewish people in
his plays. Perhaps the Kremlin feared this would arouse too
much nationalism in the Jewish people. Another assumption
is that since the State of Israel was established in 1948, the
year of his liquidation, he may have shown too much enthusi-
asm and been accused of "Zionism." In any event, the regime
was always liquidating its own children and as the "counter-
revolutionaries" and "enemies of the people" were disposed of,
most Russians could not help but jump at the sound of an auto
backfiring in the night.

Most of my theatrical friends were rather worldly devotees
of earthly pleasures. They tried by all cautious means to evade
the political fog being generated by the Communist machine.
This, inevitably, made them clannish, with a strong inclination to associate among themselves. Several of them told me
discreetly that politics and genuine theatrical art did not mix.

Although I was not part of their theatrical world, they accepted me openheartedly and sincerely as their "good American friend." This proved advantageous to me, for they regularly provided me with passes to theaters and to the ballet. I
was always thrilled by the ballet, the excitement of being in
the magnificent Bolshoi Theater, during a performance of
Swan Lake or Pushkin's *Fountain of Bakchisarai*, is almost in-

describable. There was an aura about those nights that I still feel a nostalgia for. Stalin and his court often occupied dim boxes near the stage, but even their presence could not detract from the gaiety of promenading in the foyers during the intermission, or eating in the buffet with the lovely olive-colored understudy to the leading lady at one of the city's leading theaters. I supplied her with fashion magazines from Paris and New York, in return for her theater passes. Another actress friend supplied me with passes in exchange for high-quality cosmetics and silk stockings. The barter system on a cultural level had some decided advantages.

I unfailingly became the cynosure of all eyes as I dined with one or the other of these beauties in a popular café on Pushkin Square. And one of these lovely girls, upon learning that I planned to go to Berlin for a holiday, asked me to marry her and take her along.

"Just take me to Berlin," she said. "Afterwards you need not feel any further obligation to me if you don't want to." I felt sorry that I couldn't accommodate her, but I couldn't.

A very popular actress was scheduled to go on a road tour lasting for several months. Preferring to rent her small apartment to a foreigner, she advertised its availability in the newspaper, *Evening Moscow*.

A well-known American Negro Communist, in Moscow "on business," saw the advertisement and went to see about renting the apartment. Naturally she asked him where he was employed. When he told her the Comintern, she told him to come back within two days. When he returned she expressed regrets, giving as her reason that her tour had been canceled. Later she confided to me, "I don't want any damn Communists of any color living in my flat."

The unexpectedly Bohemian behavior of one of my lovely friends resulted in my having to take a long, cold and late walk across Moscow in the dead of winter.

One night she had given a small party in her room in a

building on Tverskaya Boulevard. Three other couples and myself were present. When all my American phonograph records had been played many times over, and after the vodka and caviar had been "liquidated" and the hour become late, the guests, including myself, prepared to leave. The hostess tugged at my sleeve, quietly hinting that I need not go, and adding that no street cars or taxis were available at that hour of night anyway. I acquiesed without further ado, but after the other guests had departed, and the vodka was beginning to wear off, I asked about a certain picture on the wall.

"Oh, that's my husband," she answered.

After remarking that I did not realize she had a husband, I naturally was curious to know his whereabouts.

"He went with some friends to hunt bears three days ago," she answered nonchalantly, "and I haven't the slightest idea when he'll be returning."

With only one door and one window on a balcony three floors up from the cement sidewalk, I then and there decided that it would be the better part of prudence to bid my hospitable hostess goodnight. Facing the bitter mid-winter cold in a cross town walk was far preferable to the risk of becoming an *Ursus Americanus* for a charge of bear-shot.

CHAPTER VII

I Meet Pushkin's
Great Granddaughter

"And quicken Thou in me the breath and being of
Both fortitude and meekness, chastity and love."
—Alexander Pushkin, "Pure Men
And Women Too"

WHILE READING Moscow's popular newspaper, *Evening
Moscow*, on a white-night summer evening in 1936, I
was brought up with a start. My eyes had fallen upon a story
—surprising and intriguing to me—about Catherine Pushkin,
great-granddaughter of the celebrated poet, Alexander Pushkin.

Pushkin had always been one of my favorite men of letters
and I had read just about all his works that had been translated into English. I had even struggled with some of his un-
translated works in Russian. But I had not had the slightest
idea that any of Pushkin's direct descendants were alive and
living in Moscow, though I had already lived there for several
years.

The story also mentioned Catherine Pushkin's address,
which happened to be only four blocks from my hotel. Grab-
bing my coat and hat—and filled with emotion and great ex-
pectations—I was off post-haste for Brussovsky Pereoulok.

Finding the number I was looking for, I passed through a

gate into a large courtyard and asked an old dvornik (yard-man) where Catherine Pushkin lived. Tipping his cap, he pointed to a sub-basement apartment in a three-story red-brick building on the eastern side of the courtyard.

"Go down there," the man said, directing me to a flight of stairs, "and knock at the door on the left."

A Pushkin, a descendant of Russia's greatest poet and creator of Russia's literary language, a great-granddaughter of Alexander Pushkin, Russian nobleman and literary giant, living in sub-basement quarters? I could not help but feel the old dvornik had not fully understood my still imperfect use of the Russian language. But I followed his directions and descended the stairs.

In response to my knock, a young peach-colored woman in early thirties came to the door.

"Are you Catherine Pushkin?" I asked.

"Yes, I am Catherine Pushkin," she answered in a soft feminine voice.

After I had introduced myself, she said with charming courtesy, "Very pleasant, please come in."

She led me down a narrow, dim hallway to a single room about thirty feet square. There were two windows, one-half of them above ground and the balance below the level of the courtyard. On one side of the room stood an iron bed and on the other a sagging divan, over which hung a large portrait of Alexander Pushkin. Between the windows was an old dresser and on the floor a tattered rug. I was taken aback at finding a Pushkin living in such squalor, but I suppressed my feelings.

Catherine Pushkin had been about thirteen years old when the Revolution burst upon Russia in 1917. She was living with her aristocratic parents and attending one of Moscow's exclusive girls' finishing schools. Her parents were cultured and wealthy people, but they lost everything in the Bolshevik *coup d'état*. Catherine's further education was frustrated, and she and her parents became declassé.

But despite the fact that her education could not be completed—the new Communist regime made schooling available only for children of the toiling masses—Catherine Pushkin's bearing, manners and speech still attested to her genteel background. She was and remained a Russian gentlewoman, despite the new regime's scorn of etiquette or the observance of the accepted rules of polite society.

There was nothing Negroid about Catherine, any more than there is anything Negroid about thousands of colored women in the United States who are classified as Negroes. Her soft skin was peach-colored—something not uncommon in Russia—and her dark brown hair had a slight wave in it. Her eyes were dark brown. She was full-bosomed, had a slightly plump figure and was about five feet, five inches tall.

Our conversation on this first visit was devoted almost wholly to her great-grandfather, Alexander Pushkin, and she proved to be a rich storehouse of information about her celebrated ancestor. She was steeped in Pushkin's life and activities and was well acquainted with the history of his African ancestry. My questions seemed endless, but she seemed to enjoy answering them.

She told me the name of another of Pushkin's Moscow descendants, and it was through her that I later came to make his acquaintance and gain his friendship. It was Catherine who also directed me to all of the historic Pushkin spots in Moscow and Leningrad and this information enabled me later to follow in Pushkin's footsteps, as it were, from his birthplace to his grave.

The hours passed all too quickly, and the milky whiteness of a Moscow summer midnight lay outside before I realized the lateness of the hour. Among Catherine's last words were: "Alexander Sergeevich was dark-complexioned, a few shades lighter than you. I am so sorry that my color is so light. He would have been fond of you, I am sure."

Before I passed out into the white night, Catherine asked

me to come to see her again, at any time. I would always be welcome. I expressed my thanks, promising to call again. This promise was kept and my visits thereafter became regular, interrupted only by my subsequent marriage.

On one of my later visits Catherine called in two young boys from their play in the courtyard. She pointed to their badly-worn clothes and shoes.

"Could you possibly help these poor boys? They are relatives of mine. Perhaps some of your relatives in America could send them some clothes and shoes?" she asked.

I assured Catherine that it could be done, but I realized that to do this would probably take two or three months. Furthermore, there was no assurance that the parcel would arrive; it might be confiscated by the Moscow Post Office. So the next day I decided upon a quicker and seemingly surer method of helping the boys.

Paul Robeson had left his son in Moscow for two years at the Moscow Model School. Paul, Jr., was living with his grandmother, Mrs. Goode, in the Metropole Hotel, and though he was somewhat larger than the boys Catherine had shown me, that should make little difference. I was on good terms with the Robesons and this made my task easier. Yet I did not want to tell them that two young Russian boys—and related to a Pushkin—were sorely in need of young Paul's clothes and shoes.

Accordingly, I took another tact. Two of my neighbor's boys, I explained, were desperately in need of shoes and clothes. They were about the same size as Paul, Jr.; did young Robeson have any extra clothes or shoes that he could spare? It worked perfectly.

That same week I called on Catherine Pushkin and presented her with a fine bundle of quality clothes and shoes. No questions were asked by Catherine, and the Russian boys dressed like American school boys for a long time thereafter.

One evening Catherine Pushkin asked me if I would like to

meet Pushkin's grandson, Gregori Pushkin. I answered that I most certainly would. We walked through Trubnaya Square, turned into a side-street and came to an old white stone building in two rooms of which lived Gregori Pushkin. He was then about seventy-five years old, gray-haired, sallow-complexioned and wizened.

He greeted me in courtly fashion, in the manner of old-school and cultured Russians. "I have heard much about American Negroes, but this is the first time I have had the pleasure and honor of meeting one," he remarked, as he bowed me to a comfortable chair.

He soon had his samovar boiling and tea was served—with the inevitable vodka, caviar and black bread.

Like several of Pushkin's descendants, Gregori Pushkin, though now declassé under the Soviet regime, had had a distinguished career in the Russian Army. And inasmuch as Catherine had told me about all there was to know about their celebrated ancestor, I showed interest in Gregori Pushkin's career.

He had graduated from a famous Russian military school, had served as an officer during the Russo-Japanese War of 1905. During World War I he had commanded the Pechersky Regiment on the Austro-Hungarian-Russian front and had been decorated for heroism and bravery by Czar Nicholas II. He was silent—perhaps understandably—about his military activities after the Bolsheviks seized power in 1917.

When I asked Gregori Pushkin what he thought Alexander Pushkin's attitude toward the Soviet regime would be if he were alive today, he became taciturn and suggested that I decide that question for myself. He, like most of Russia's former aristocrats and nobility, seemed clearly to realize that despite his distinguished ancestry and advanced age any "deviationist" or "subversive" remarks would subject him to the merciless wrath of the Secret Police.

From my researches in the archives on the life and times of

Alexander Pushkin, my conviction is that Pushkin would have
been thoroughly unhappy and disgruntled if he had lived under Stalin's regime. A rebel he was, perhaps even a revolutionary, but Pushkin called himself a "singer of freedom" and
wrote that "freedom boils in my heart." He was no conformist,
despite the fact that he lived in an age of harsh, authoritarian
rule and during it his own writings were constantly censored,
sometimes even by Czar Nicholas himself. He was deeply involved in oppositionist politics and some of his closest friends
were leaders of the secret oppositionist *Welfare Union* and its
southern branch, the *League of Felicity*.

But his revolutionary poems and biting epigrams were always directed against dictatorial and tyrannical rule. They
played a great inspirational role among the leaders and members of the secret societies, and when several members of the
societies were arrested by the Czarist police, they were found
to be in possession of Pushkin's revolutionary verses.

At the time of the Decembrist uprising in St. Petersburg in
1825 (so called because it occurred in December), Czar Nicholas ordered Pushkin brought into his presence. Pushkin com-
plied fearlessly.

"Would you have taken part in the uprising of December
14th if you had been in St. Petersburg?" the Czar asked.

"Undoubtedly, Sire," Pushkin answered. "All of my friends
were in on the plot, and I could not have done otherwise than
take part in it. Only my absence from the city prevented me."

The dossiers of the Czar's Third Department (Secret Police) recorded that "Pushkin heaped scorn in public places on
the army and even on the Government" and that Pushkin once
remarked publicly that "a bear was a kinder creature than the
Czar." Once in the Imperial Theater in St. Petersburg, Pushkin prominently displayed a large picture of the Duc de Berri,
liberal and benevolent son of Charles X of France, who was
assassinated by reactionaries in 1820. It bore the warning in-
scription: "A lesson to Kings." And in his poem *Volost* (Free-

dom) Pushkin wrote of the Czar: "Despotic miscreant, Thee and Thy Throne I hate."

No, I have strong doubts that Alexander Pushkin, lover of freedom and protagonist of human rights and human dignity, could have escaped liquidation had he lived under the Stalin regime. And it is certain that had he openly called a bear a kinder creature than Stalin—well, the bearish Stalin would have smothered him into oblivion.

During the years I knew Catherine Pushkin, one of my closest Russian friends, I found her to be possessed of characteristics similar to her celebrated ancestor—kindness and affability, simplicity and honesty. But whereas Alexander Pushkin was deeply interested and involved in the politics of his time, Catherine Pushkin—perhaps as a cautionary measure—showed no outward interest in contemporary political affairs.

Was Alexander Pushkin—Russia's greatest and most beloved poet—a Negro?

There has been much misinformation and confusion about Pushkin's African racial connection. To the Russians he was, and is, a Russian; American Negroes, pardonably and understandably enough, call him a Negro.

Pushkin's father was Count Sergei Pushkin, white scion of an ancient noble Russian family. His mother was called the "lovely creole."

America's leading Pushkinist, Professor Ernest J. Simmons, denies that Pushkin inherited any Negro blood. In his biography of the great poet, Professor Simmons claims that Pushkin's first African ancestor in Russia, Abram Hannibal, "was an Abyssinian and not a Negro." Professor Simmons even repeats the old fable that the Ethiopians belong "to the Caucasian division of races."

All attempts to give Pushkin a wholly "Caucasian" family tree contradict both Peter the Great and Pushkin. In a message to the Russian diplomatic envoy in Constantinople early in the eighteenth century, Peter the Great requested him to send him "a young Negro with good talent."

Pushkin himself was always proud of the Negro strain in his ancestry. At the age of 27, ten years before his death, he began writing a historical novel based on the life of his African great-grandfather. Its title was to be *The Negro of Peter the Great.*

I recall arguing the point of Pushkin's Negro ancestry with Professor Simmons on one of his visits to Russia in the late 1930's. We reached no accord, with Professor Simmons adhering to his Abyssinian-Caucasian descent theory. As an American, I recollect telling him he should be the last person to try to deny that Alexander Pushkin was of Negro ancestry.

Indeed, had Pushkin lived in America he would certainly have been classified by the United States Census Bureau as a Negro. There are countless colored persons living in America who are far lighter in skin color than Pushkin was and who have equally direct infusions of Caucasian blood. Yet, in America they are classified as Negroes.

Abram Hannibal, Pushkin's great-grandfather, is known to have been black and to have had woolly hair, and a leading European Pushkinist of Russian descent, Henri Troyat, has written that Hannibal had "thick lips and kinkyish hair." Of Pushkin, the same authority wrote that he had a "mass of tight curls on his head and wide nostrils."

I have visited the area in northern Ethiopia from which Hannibal came. I saw no people there even remotely resembling Caucasians; all around me were black people with woolly hair.

It is quite possible that young Hannibal, growing to manhood in Russia among nobles and aristocrats, may have attempted to claim Caucasian ancestry, though this seems doubtful. He had no reason to. What is more probable is that he may have claimed to be better born than he was.

In some parts of Africa and in most Eastern countries many

claim ancestry from some distant legendary hero, important family or aristocratic progenitor. Some non-European royalty claims, however circuitous, to have family roots going back to Mohammed, founder of the Islamic religion. Even in old Russia some of the great Russian nobles, no doubt for "status" purposes, claimed a legendary and illustrious German named Radsha as one of the roots to their family trees.

Another example that has some pertinence exists today in Abram's native country. Ethiopia's monarchs—without any proof other than a legend—claimed direct descent from King Solomon through the Queen of Sheba. Emperor Haile Selassie, perpetuating the legend, claims that he, too, is descended directly from that liaison.

When it is recalled that Solomon lived one thousand years before the Christian era and that Ethiopia has had hundreds of Kings since then—some of them from disparate tribes and all having kept many concubines—it is certainly far-fetched that so much undiluted geneology could have resulted from that one ancient love-nest of the King of Israel.

Such "status-seeking" may have had some bearing on Hannibal's assumption of the family name of Hannibal in Russia in 1730. During his youth, the young African must have heard the name of the great Carthaginian North African general and laid claim to ancestral ties with him.

Some sources claimed—and both Hannibal and Pushkin supported the claim—that Hannibal's father had been an Abyssinian Prince, a royal vassal of the Ottoman Turks. This perhaps was another effort aimed at giving Hannibal "status" and should be looked upon with a certain amount of skepticism. It is highly doubtful that the Turks would have sought out the son of a Prince.

In tracing Pushkin's African geneology, one must go back to the year 1705. Peter the Great was on the throne of Russia; the Ottoman Empire controlled the northern coastal region of Abyssinia.

Inland from that coast, on the banks of the Mareb River, is a region that is today known as Eritrea. It was not unusual in those days for young Negro boys to be captured and shipped to Turkey to become eunuchs in the harems of the Turkish Sultan, his Grand Vizier or other Turkish potentates. Many young Negroes were destined to grow up and become members of the Janizary (the Sultan's Guard).

When a Turkish vessel set sail northwards in the Red Sea, in 1705, it had on board a seven-year old Negro boy named Abram (I have been unable to find the family name in the records). About one year after the young boy's arrival in Constantinople, the Russian envoy, Count Raguzinsky, in response to Peter the Great's request for a young Negro entered into negotiations with Turkish officials and delivered him to Peter the Great in Moscow in 1706.

This, in brief, is the story of how Alexander Pushkin's African progenitor left his native Africa and reached distant Russia.

Peter the Great took a great liking to the young Negro, and this later turning into deep affection. Abram was quickly attached to the Czar's entourage, slept in his private apartment, and became his confidant and private secretary, handling secret messages between the Czar and his Ministers.

When Peter the Great had Abram christened in a Russian Pravo-Slav church in 1707, he stood as Abram's godfather. The wife of the King of Poland served as his godmother. Abram was christened with the name of Peter, after his royal patron, but he never liked the name and later in life assumed the name of Abram Petrovich Hannibal.

The young Negro boy became so attached to his patron, and his patron to him, that when Peter the Great made a royal visit to France in 1717, he included Abram in his retinue. Abram was not to see Russia again for six years, for the Czar left him in a French military school, with all expenses paid. Later, after entering the French military-engineering school at Metz, he became so proficient in his studies that he was awarded the rank of Captain in the French Army.

As a dashing young military officer, Abram gained entree to the best salons of Paris, where he became a great favorite, especially among the French ladies. He found life in France so much to his liking that when Peter the Great demanded that he return to Russia, Abram found numerous excuses for extending his stay. Finally, his excuses were exhausted and in 1723 he returned to Russia. Peter the Great was delighted at the return of his young protégé, Russia's first fully educated military engineer and fortifications expert.

Peter the Great died in 1725, but not before he had appointed Abram to a high engineering post in the Russian Army, and made him teacher of mathematics to the heir apparent to the Russian throne. Shortly after the death of Peter the Great, Abram was shipped off to the Russian-Chinese border to engage in fortifications work. But when Empress Anna Ivanova ascended the throne in 1730, she recalled Abram to St. Petersburg and appointed him to the high-ranking military post of captain-engineer at the fortress of Pernau, in the Russian Baltic.

During his stay in France, Abram had evidently developed a keen eye for beautiful women, and his eyes now fell upon a beautiful young girl of Greek descent named Evdokia, daughter of a Greek captain in the Russian Navy, Andrei Dioper. The girl disliked Abram and had no desire to become his wife, remarking in an aside that he was "a Negro, not of our kind."

However, back in those days, the final word in such matters rested with the parents, and Captain Dioper granted Abram's request for the hand of his daughter. Abram and Evdokia were married in 1731, and it began to look as if Hannibal's descendants would be of African-Greek descent.

But the marriage did not last long. Evdokia was somewhat of a flirt—not uncommon in those days—and Hannibal accused her of infidelity. They separated in 1732 and as was the custom of the time—especially when the charge was made by such an important person as Hannibal—Evdokia was arrested, but not before Hannibal had soundly thrashed her and secluded her in a military stockade.

Pushkin, in one of his light moments, remarked that the separation resulted from Evdokia giving birth to a white baby girl. But this allegation was without foundation, for during their life together, no child was born to Hannibal and Evdokia.

Hannibal then married Christina Scheberg, daughter of a Captain of German origin in the Russian service. It was rumored at the time that while Hannibal was accusing Evdokia of infidelity, he himself was trysting with Christina.

Great compatibility and attachment marked the married life of Hannibal and Christina. Eleven children were born to them, among them Ossip Hannibal, who was to become the father of Alexander Pushkin's mother, Nadezhda Hannibal, the "lovely creole."

Christina Hannibal died in her seventy-sixth year; Abram Hannibal lived on until his eighty-fourth year. He died honored, wealthy and the possessor of the highest decorations that Russian rulers could award.

I have not attempted to "prove" that because Abram Hannibal was a Negro, Alexander Pushkin must also have been a Negro. Pushkin was born, felt, thought and lived as a Russian. Nor would I be so rash to attempt to attribute Pushkin's genius to his Negro blood. To attempt to solve the riddle of genius is an impossible exercise.

CHAPTER VIII

Variations on a Color Theme

"What fools these mortals be . . ."
—Spencer

IF I HAD BEEN LOOKING for racial equality in Russia, I found it so abundant that it proved, in my opinion, to amount almost to racial inequality. This requires some explanation. If a Negro was standing in line at a shop, some Russian was sure to tug him by the arm and lead him to the front of the line. If it was a matter of a dance with a Russian girl, a Russian man would always give way. Upon entering any building, Negroes would always be given precedence. In a barber shop or restaurant, although a Russian might long have been waiting his turn, he would always be willing to relinquish it to a Negro. Thus, Negroes who were looking only for racial equality found themselves given the full treatment of racial inequality in reverse.

Seeing this racial inequality in action, but in reverse order to what I had seen in America, proved intriguing and pleasant. In all my years in Russia I had only one slightly unpleasant racial incident that did not involve a Russian at all. Indeed, I am not absolutely certain it even involved race. Anyway, here is what happened:

I was bound for Leningrad to do some additional research work on Alexander Pushkin in the Pushkin House at the Academy of Sciences. My ticket on the de luxe *wagon lit* (sleeping car) of the Red Arrow, Russia's crack train and the only one that had a record of consistently running on time, called for a lower berth in number 5 compartment.

Russian ticket offices sell accommodations on the basis of first come, first served, disregarding race, color, sex or nationality. Under this arrangement, it often happened that men and women found themselves holding tickets for the same compartment, though perfect strangers, and no puritanical objections were ever raised.

I had more than once traveled in a four-berth compartment containing two men (one of them me) and two women. And I have more than once even had a Russian woman as my sole traveling companion in a compartment with not the slightest raising of eyebrows by the woman or by any other passenger.

On this particular summer evening, I was sitting comfortably in my compartment reading the *Evening Moscow*. Shortly before eight o'clock a "red cap" appeared at the compartment door, pushed two suitcases in and started to lift them up onto the baggage rack. Over his shoulders I saw two disapproving eyes peering into the compartment.

"Hold on! There must be some mistake," a woman's voice exclaimed in English.

"Your ticket says compartment number 5, Madam," the porter said.

"Then there must be something wrong," the woman remarked.

The porter shrugged his shoulders and left the suitcases on the floor, suggesting to the woman that she go and see the conductor. Returning with this gentleman, my fellow passenger repeated her remarks about an error having been made.

"Let me see your ticket, Madam," the conductor suggested,

and also requested mine. Comparing the two tickets and the number over the compartment door, he told her he could see nothing wrong.

"But I must have another compartment! I can't . . ." she remarked, without completing what I knew she meant to say.

"Madam, this train *never* has any vacant berths," the conductor answered coldly.

The woman persisted in making a fool of herself, and demanded that something be done or she would see the stationmaster. The conductor informed her that the stationmaster had nothing to do with issuing tickets.

"You have your correct ticket, Madam. The train leaves in five minutes," the conductor told her and returned to the outer platform.

The woman was middle-aged and rather plump. She had slightly graying hair, blue eyes and a ruddy complexion. Overall, she struck me as being plain and my guess was that she might be a school teacher far from home in a country whose mores were far different from those she was accustomed to. Then, too, perhaps my brown color was responsible for her perturbed reaction.

"Aren't you from the United States?" she asked.

"Madam, whether or not I am from the United States is of no importance. You are not in the United States now," I answered politely, without any show of annoyance.

For though she could not bring herself to be a civilized lady in an un-Christian and atheistic country, I was determined not to be rude and to demonstrate to her that her would-be compartment companion was very much a gentleman.

She dragged her suitcases out into the corridor in a huff, just as the Red Arrow glided slowly out of the shed. I lit my pipe and returned to my newspaper.

Shortly afterwards, the conductor—the same one—returned to collect our tickets.

"I hope you have a pleasant and comfortable trip, *Gospodin*.

We are due in Leningrad at eight o'clock in the morning," he said politely.

Around ten o'clock I closed the compartment door, undressed and crawled into my berth. The woman was still standing in the corridor between her two suitcases. I did not lock the door; after all, the woman had a valid ticket that entitled her to the vacant berth.

The porter, a Russian woman, came along shortly after this, and through the closed door I heard her questioning the standing passenger.

"Madam, it is getting late. Don't you want to retire?"

"No!" came the gruff answer.

The Red Arrow rolled along smoothly through the lovely Russian white night, arriving in Leningrad sharply at eight o'clock the next morning. I had slept well in my first class compartment, with washroom and toilet all to myself, though I had paid for only half of it.

Before getting off, I managed to have a word with the porter.

"What did my fellow passenger do last night?" I asked.

"She sat all night on one of her suitcases. And as she was leaving a few minutes ago she gave me a mean look and said, 'this is a hell of a country!' "

I did not hate or despise the woman; I pitied her. Perhaps some carnal thoughts had been racing through her prejudiced mind, some unjustified vision of being raped in the quiet Russian night. Actually, had she shown any degree of good sense or manners, I would have been quite ready to surrender my lower berth to her. And I'm sure I would have slept soundly throughout the night without any sensual thoughts of her stretched out in the lower berth beneath me.

With my mission to Leningrad completed, I bought a ticket on the Red Arrow for my return to Moscow. Shortly before departure time a young Russian woman appeared puffing at the door of my compartment. She was carrying her own baggage.

"I couldn't find a porter. Will you please help me put my bags up? You know, I almost missed the train."

Russians are a very inquisitive people and my fellow passenger wanted to know what country I came from, where I worked, what had brought me to Leningrad from Moscow and whether my trip had been pleasant.

"Quite pleasant, with one exception," I told her.

Naturally, she was curious to know what that exception had been. So I related to her the somewhat amusing story of the woman who refused to occupy the compartment with me.

"The decadent bourgeois swine! That's the kind of misanthrope that capitalism spawns," my companion exclaimed.

With this, I dismissed the matter from my mind and thought that I would hear no more about it. But I was mistaken, for the conductor on the train from Moscow, or someone, in any event had apparently reported the incident to "proper channels."

Three days after my arrival in Moscow, a reporter from the trade union newspaper *Trud* contacted me about the incident. I told him the facts just as they had happened, and the next day *Trud* published a story with Marxist ideological overtones and anti-capitalist embellishments that expanded the incident out of all proportion to its importance.

About a week after my return to Moscow, a friend of mine told me of an incident that was certainly more typical of what usually happens when racial incidents are instigated by foreigners in Russia.

Tamara Lavrova, a comely 19-year old blond friend of his, had studied English at the Institute of Foreign Languages. Because of the large number of European and American engineers and technicians working in Russia, interpreters were in great demand by the Soviet Government to work with such foreigners.

Tamara had been assigned to serve as an interpreter for a well-paid American electrical engineer. She found her work pleasant and satisfactory, but socially she had other interests. One of these was a colored American technician then employed at a Russian Factory. The two often spent their evenings dancing in the leading hotels, which were mainly patronized by Americans and other foreigners.

One evening, while dining in the restaurant of the Savoy Hotel, Tamara said to her colored companion, "See that man at the corner table? He is your countryman, and I work with him. But I am beginning to dislike him."

This naturally aroused the curiosity of her companion, who wanted to know why.

"One day he told me he wanted to have a few serious words with me," Tamara answered. "And can you imagine what he wanted to tell me?"

Her companion shrugged. "Miss Tamara, you are a very pretty and efficient girl. I find your work quite satisfactory. But several times I have seen you in the company of a Negro. I personally don't approve of this and I tell you quite frankly that if it continues I won't find it possible to let you continue working for me. Can you imagine such foolish talk?"

Tamara's colored American companion, of course, was curious to know what Tamara's reaction was to this feckless attempt at racial prejudice.

"Naturally, I became quite angry," Tamara replied. "I told him bluntly that it was none of his damned business whom I associated with socially. I almost laughed in the silly fool's face when he hinted that he was afraid he wouldn't find it possible to let me continue working for him. I made it very clear that I was employed by the Soviet Government and that he was not my employer, didn't pay my salary and couldn't dismiss me. I also warned him that if he ever made any such racist remarks to me again, I should have to consider reporting him to my government. And if he didn't know what that could mean, let me tell you; you might be given forty-eight hours to leave Russia!"

I knew this engineer personally and was aware that he was earning a salary twice as large as he had been earning in America before the depression rendered him jobless. With unemployment still widespread in the United States, there was little likelihood that he could find work if he were forced to leave Russia.

Tamara had evidently brought him to the realization that his efforts to indoctrinate her in American racial mores could mean a quick exit visa for him. Until the end of his contract, Tamara told me afterwards, he carefully guarded his tongue and never mentioned anything racial to her again. Apparently he resigned himself to the fact that it would be useless and risky to try to create a "problem" where none existed.

While there were a number of Negroes from the United States in Russia during my fourteen years there, I can't really remember any experience that was more humorous than Dick Williams first encounter with the professional Russian woman. Dick who was an electrical engineer, trained at Columbia University in New York City, came to Russia shortly after I did. He hadn't been in Moscow long when he developed sharp attacks of arthritic pains in both his thighs. Since he knew no Russian, he asked me to accompany him to the big polyclinic on Petrovka Street for a check-up. I could act as his interpreter.

Now, most doctors were, and are, women in Russia. The expert on Dick's ailment happened to be a comely woman doctor (I shall call her Dr. Mila) of 40; Dick was in his late 40's. When we were called into the examination room, Dick found himself facing Dr. Mila and two women assistants.

After explaining his difficulty, with me interpreting, Dr. Mila said she would have to make a thorough medical examination.

"Take off your shirt," she said. Off went Dick's undershirt.

"Now your pants," she asked.

"Now tell the Gospodin (Gentleman) to take off his shoes, socks—and drawers and lie on the table," she asked me.

Dick gave a faraway and quizzical look.

"I am merely interpreting, Dick," I said.

Soon there was Dick sprawled on the table, absolutely nude, with three women ready to begin the examination.

I wanted to go out into the waiting room while the doctor and her assistants worked Dick over. But the doctor said she would have to ask Dick some questions and requested that I stay.

Soft hands pressed, probed and glided over Dick's thighs, legs and buttocks. Once in a while he cast sly glances at me.

After all this was over, Dr. Mila told Dick he would need a thorough and regular regime of therapeutics, and would have to return to the clinic for treatment at frequent intervals. This delayed his departure to the plant he had been assigned to by the Heavy Industry Commissariat.

Some kind of rapport of a non-medical nature must have been established between Dick and Dr. Mila for they were married within six months, with Dick moving into her apartment near the polyclinic.

About a year later a son was born and began developing eyes that were distinctly of the almond-eyed type typical of the Mongols of some regions in Siberia. Dick mentioned this physical characteristic to me with some misgiving and said he did not know of any Asiatic blood in his ancestry.

"But Dick," I said, "you need to read up on Russian history. You know that the Asiatic Tartar hordes invaded and occupied Russia back in the thirteenth century and later ruled the country for something like 200 years. There inescapably was a heavy intermixture of blood; it has happened on a large scale in our own country, as you must know. Even today the Russians show physical traits of that Tartar admixture, and this could account for your child being almond-eyed."

My historical and ethnological reminder appeared to have little effect on Dick.

"Yes, I know about that Tartar invasion of long ago," Dick

said. "But I also know of a Chinese laundryman today just around the corner from our apartment. The child's yellowish color I can understand, but the eyes . . . !"

Despite my urgings and reminders that he had a fine and intelligent wife who was a respected member of a learned profession, Dick could not reconcile himself to his child's Oriental appearance. They separated, she remaining in Moscow, and he fulfilling his commitment as an electrical engineer in the Cossack Country of the Ukraine.

Others among the American Negro expatriate population included Robert Robinson, a fine tolerance tool maker from Detroit; George Tynes, an agriculturist from Wilberforce, Lloyd Patterson, an interior decorator from Hampton, Virginia who had come over with the Black and White group, and Wayland Rudd.

It was a long jump from Roanoke, Virginia and Wilberforce University to Moscow, but George Tynes made the transition with little or no difficulty. In 1935 when he came out of Wilberforce with a degree in agriculture and unable to find employment in his field, George came to Russia with the idea of utilizing Booker T. Washington's "cast down your bucket" theory, leaving out only the "where you are" portion. He knew not one word of the Russian language, nothing about the habits and customs of the country, and for years he worked as the chief zoologist on a vast collective farm just outside the Crimean capital city of Simferopol. Today, I understand he is technical director of a game preserve, in a rural area on the outskirts of Moscow. He is considered one of the leading authorities on fish and ducks in the Soviet Union. He and his Russian wife have one son, she has a grown son by a previous marriage.

Lloyd Patterson, the art student from Hampton Institute who had specialized in interior decorating, had never been able to use his profession in America. He often made the statement that the closest he got to working at his trade in Westfield,

New Jersey, his home town, was whitewashing fences. Patterson married a well-known Russian artist named Vera, and they became parents of three sons, one of whom I understand has graduated with honors from the Naval Academy, and is now a commissioned officer in the Russian Navy. Unfortunately, Lloyd Patterson died quite suddenly, while on a trip away from Moscow, in the early forties.

Robert Robinson, a native of Kingston, Jamaica, but a naturalized American citizen and graduate of Cass Technical School in Detroit, came to Moscow under a one year contract to the Soviet Government to instruct young workers in toolgrinding. Robinson, who had been an employee of Ford Motor Company was a quiet, scholarly bachelor who served for four years as a deputy in the Moscow Soviet, and as a result ran into trouble with the U. S. State Department. Upon his election to the Moscow Soviet (the local legislative body) the American Embassy in Moscow wrote to him advising him to return to the U. S. When he refused, he was denied an extension of his passport. He has been in Moscow ever since. Some of his instruments may have contributed to the advance of Russia in the "Sputnik race."

Wayland Rudd, a big, amiable black fellow, was one of the Negroes who had come over with the Black and White film group and decided to remain in Russia when the rest of the group returned to the states. Wayland had had considerable stage experience before coming to Russia, appearing with the Hedgerow Players group in Philadelphia and in the New York company of the original *Porgy and Bess* and *Blood Stream*. He had a good voice and after the film fiasco his overwhelming desire was to become a leading actor on the Russian stage. He wanted particularly to play the role of *Othello,* as Ira Aldridge had done in Russia some sixty years before. Unfortunately this wish was not to be fulfilled. He had little real success as an actor, and later studied at the Institute of Cinematography with the idea of becoming a film director. As far as he got in

Russian films was playing the role of "Nigger Jim" in the Adventures of Huckleberry Finn, and other minor roles in films requiring an exotic character.

For a brief period he was married to an American white girl of good family who came to Russia, but she returned to the States and he married a Bulgarian girl by whom he had a son. He died in Moscow during the mid 1950's having discovered that the road of the thespian is a rocky one, whether it be in Moscow or Broadway, U.S.A.

CHAPTER IX

I See the New Soviet Constitution Born

"The most democratic constitution in the world."
—Stalin on the new constitution, 1936

IN 1935, when my contract with the post office expired, I had not renewed it. One reason for this was that since 1932 I had been sending news dispatches to the Negro Press in America. During the next three years, my pieces began to appear with some regularity in such papers as the *Chicago Defender* and the *Afro-American,* as well as in *Crisis Magazine,* the organ of the N.A.A.C.P. If I was ever going to make the break to being a full-time journalist, now seemed to be the time.

And so, on the bitter-cold evening of December 5, 1936, I found myself comfortably seated in the press box of the snow-white, high vaulted St. Andrew's Hall in the Great Kremlin Palace. Russian Czars and Czarinas formerly moved about in regal pomp and circumstance in this great hall, and I could not but wonder if their shades might be looking down upon the spectacle than being enacted in their former imperial domicile.

My press card, which had to be accompanied by a special

ticket for this occasion, had been closely examined at least five times by uniformed NKVD men before I was finally admitted to the press box. I was stopped first at the gate in the Kremlin wall, at another gate opening into the palace courtyard, at the outer entrance into the lower floor of the palace, as I stepped off an elevator on an upper floor, and finally at a door opening into the press box. Ranged along the same level as the press box, were the packed loges of the foreign Diplomatic Corps. Below in the vast hall, were the members of the Eighth All-Union Congress of the Soviets. Stalin and his Politburo and Central Executive Committee of the Communist Party were seated in special rows to the left and right of the dais and behind it.

All present had come to witness the ratification and adoption of a new constitution. The 1936 Constitution had been preceded by the 1918 and 1924 Constitutions, not to mention the document which Emperor Nicholas II had been pressured into issuing in 1905 under the name of the October Manifesto. The 1936 Constitution, Stalin proclaimed: ". . . preserves the regime of the dictatorship of the proletariat just as it also preserves without change the leading position of the Communist Party of the U.S.S.R."

The party leaders had first decided to create the new constitution back in the winter of 1934–35. Orders to implement this decision reached the Eighth Congress of Soviets in February 1935 and a drafting commission of 31 members had gone to work immediately under Stalin's direction.

The new constitutional draft received the widest possible circulation. It was reported that sixty million copies were circulated all over the U.S.S.R., and under party direction carefully studied and discussed. One hundred and fifty-four thousand suggestions for modification or changes were made. A mere 43 were adopted. This was the document that the Eighth Congress of Soviets had been called into extraordinary session to adopt. This was the document that Stalin proclaimed "the only thoroughly democratic constitution in the world."

The veteran revolutionaries who were present as members of the Eighth Congress were either satisfied that this was true, or dared not dissent, for the constitution was adopted unanimously with only a handful of editorial changes.

Basking in the reflected glory of Stalin's constitutional *tour de force*, I now wonder how many realized that their days were numbered, that they would face Stalin's firing squads during the next two years on charges of being "counter-revolutionaries," "enemies of the people," "Trotskyites or Bukharinites."

Klieg lights accentuated the milky whiteness of the hall. Photographers, all Russians, moved here and there making a documentary film of the "constituent assembly." Secret Police agents, all dressed alike, thereby making them easily recognizable, loitered at strategic points, mostly near the doors of the hall.

I peered down on a mosaic of all the nationalities of the polyglot Soviet Union—"nationality" in the Russian language meaning race and not citizenship. The Soviet Press wrote that some of them from the northern fringes of the country had begun their journey by Husky dog teams or reindeer, while others had come on horseback from the deserts of Central Asia. Still others had ridden the Trans-Siberian Railroad for several days.

There were men and women, old, middle-aged and young. Horny-handed collective farm peasants from Central Russia and the Ukraine were juxtaposed with Mongolian-faced, black-haired cattle breeders and cotton raisers from Turkestan; flat-faced, flaxen-haired office employees and factory workers from Moscow and Leningrad merged with poker-faced party functionaries.

Of the 2,016 delegates—workers and peasants, office employees, members of the "intelligentsia"—seventy-two per cent were members of the Communist Party. Even if a secret vote on adopting the new constitution had been taken the Communists were assured of an overwhelming majority.

Many of the delegates from outlying national minority regions did not even understand the Russian language and there was no time for translating all the proceedings into all the language groups represented. Some of the Asiatic members I spotted were actually asleep in their seats.

One of the most remarkable features of this "Constitutional Assembly" was that there was absolutely no controversy or debate. This was perhaps the first time in the history of constitutional processes that no differences of opinion were ever expressed. But there were endless fiery speeches—all in favor of the new constitution *in toto* and endless eulogies of Stalin, "Father of the new constitution." Joining lustily in the handclapping and hosannas to Stalin was Nikita Khrushchev, then an important, though not very big wheel in the Communist Party apparatus.

Speaker after speaker mounted the rostrum with paeans of praise for the new charter. It was compared and contrasted with bourgeois-capitalist constitutions—particularly the American Constitution—which were full of empty promises and deceptions.

"Only our Socialist society, under the leadership of Tovarisch Stalin and the Communist Party, could give the people such a democratic constitution," one speaker declared with fervor. "Our constitution is not an empty promise for the future, but is the expression of an existing fact," exhorted another.

The ancient ceiling of St. Andrew's Hall echoed the words "democratic" and "Stalin" as thunderous applause punctuated speech after speech.

The fact that there was no controversy or debate most likely was not accidental. I learned later from a reliable source that every speech had been censored in advance by a special Censorship Committee. Besides, there was nothing to debate; the new Constitution was already an untouchable *fait accompli.* The members of the Congress of the Soviets, it was obvious, had been summoned merely as a rubber stamp.

Neither the members of the Congress nor anyone else among the Soviet people had had any decisive part in the making of the new constitution. True, the impending new charter had been widely publicized in the press and on the radio and party functionaries had lectured about it at numerous meetings. But this had been done merely to give the impression that the people were somehow taking part in its making.

I have often since pondered how to reconcile the "world's most democratic constitution" with the fact that only one political party is permitted in Russia and no criticism or opposition to that party is tolerated.

I have read countless times in Soviet publications that "the Soviet people are rallied tightly around the Communist Party." But if this be so, I often asked myself, then why this fear of other political parties? One would think they would be permitted if for no other reason than to demonstrate to the world how easily they would be eliminated by the usual 99.8 percent of the votes that the Communist Party candidates are said regularly to receive. Under such an overwhelming vote, other political parties would naturally wither away.

At the close of the Congress, I jotted down the following in my notebook: "The fine promises in the new constitution sound very good. It now remains to be seen whether they will be put into practice." And when I wrote this I had in mind precisely those articles dealing with democratic freedoms and human rights. Perhaps, I thought, those articles will bring an appreciable relaxation of the arbitrary and draconic rule that I had been witnessing for the past four years, though I doubted it.

I have often read or heard it said that the Russians have always lived under oppressive and autocratic rule, hence they can never have any real conception or appreciation of democratic freedoms and rights. But I cannot wholly bring myself to subscribe to this. For to do so would be equivalent to saying that the American colonies did not want freedom and independence from autocratic British rule; the slaves in the American South had no desire for emancipation; or that backward peoples have no interest in improving their standards of living —because they had had no experience with anything different. Cicero wrote long ago: "Liberty is rendered more precious by recollections of servitude."

In my contacts with Russian friends, I observed that their deepest interest in the new constitution was in those articles dealing with democratic, human rights. When the official text of the new charter was published, the most widely read and studied sections were Articles 124 and 125—guaranteeing freedom of religious worship, freedom of speech, freedom of the press, and freedom of assembly, such as mass meetings, street processions and demonstrations.

It was thought in some circles that the Communist rulers were taking a calculated risk in promulgating these democratic guarantees. But those who thought so evidently overlooked the fact that the Communist Party still retained at its disposal the ubiquitous, omniscient Soviet Secret Police. Many Russians who took the new constitutional guarantees too literally were to rue their carelessness.

As the "world's most democratic Constitution," as Stalin had proclaimed, the new Soviet charter appeared to me and some of my colleagues to have certain constitutional weaknesses. Unlike the American Constitution, the new Soviet Constitution contained no right of the people *to petition the government for redress of grievances* (Article I, Amendment to the Constitution of the United States). And I looked in vain for one of the most cherished protections of democratic constitutions— the writ of *habaes corpus*. Furthermore, the people could never "throw the rascals out" in the next election, because only hand-picked Communist candidates were allowed on the ballot.

And we foreigners who were well-acquainted with Russian reality were wary of the guarantees of "freedom of assembly, including the holding of mass meetings and street demonstrations" (article 125).

During my pre-Constitution years I had seen some of the world's largest mass meetings and massive street demonstrations in the streets and squares of Moscow. But they were never in protest over anything and after the new constitution was adopted I was to find that nothing had changed. The meetings, processions and demonstrations were, as before, not spontaneously organized by the people; they were the same old compulsory window dressing initiated and organized by the Communist Party or Communist-controlled organizations. *Status quo ante.*

When I arrived in Russia, if freedom of the press existed it was only for the Communist Party and its affiliated organizations such as the Communist Youth League, the trade unions, etc. The new Constitution, despite its guarantee of freedom of the press as a "fundamental right" of every Soviet citizen, was to do nothing to change this.

It was impossible for Soviet citizens to make use of this "guarantee" and to enjoy such a "fundamental right"—so long as all presses and paper mills, ink and paper suppliers were under the strict administration and control of the Communist Party and the Soviet Government.

I lived in Russia for ten years after adoption of the Soviet Constitution and I failed to observe any change in this policy or any relaxing of the ban against news from the outside, democratic world.

Even as late as 1956, from abroad, I felt certain that most of the Russian people would have liked to read the United Nations report on the situation in Hungary. But its publication in Russia was banned. Who issued the ban? What happened to the guaranteed "freedom of the press" promised in the new Soviet constitution? Another *status quo ante.*

Although I had seen Stalin many times from a distance—atop Lenin's Mausoleum on Red Square, in his dimly-lit box at the Bolshoi Theater and at previous sessions of the Soviet Congress in the Kremlin—I had never had the opportunity of getting a look at him close-up. The Constitution Congress was to offer me my first and last chance. It required some risky "gate-crashing."

I had learned from a Russian journalist that at the close of the congress Stalin would not leave through the side-door by which he had entered, but would pass through the meeting hall and enter the delegates' lounge adjoining it. But this lounge was out-of-bounds for non-delegates, let alone representatives of the foreign press, and furthermore there was no visible stairway or access leading down to it. Yet I was determined somehow to get down into that lounge. How?

I noticed what appeared to be a well-camouflaged door in one of the wooden panels of the upstairs press lounge. I pushed this panel; it did not move. Then I tried moving it to the left and it slid open, revealing a dim, curving staircase leading downwards. For all I knew it might lead down into some old secret Czarist dungeon. But I decided to take a chance.

Moving carefully downwards, I began to feel that I must by now have passed the main floor and would surely come out in the basement. Suddenly, my heel caught on one of the treads and downwards I rolled until stopped by some obstruction. A door opened and out I rolled.

An officer in the uniform of the MVD was sitting at a desk behind a railing opposite, and he glared at me cold, perhaps thinking. "What the hell. . . ."

"I want to see Tovarish Stalin," I entreated, showing him my press card and special pass as proof that I at least had been admitted legitimately into the Kremlin.

He took off his cap, scratched his head, saluted and waved me in the direction of the delegates' lounge.

I found the spacious, paneled lounge empty, except for

a few uniformed and non-uniformed Secret Police agents. I expected them to question me about my presence there, but they paid me very little attention. I presumed that they reasoned, like the officer at the bottom of the stairs, that if I had gained entry into the lounge, then somebody in authority must certainly have permitted me to.

The reason no one was in the lounge was because the delegates were still inside the meeting hall, since under the rules of precedence, nobody could precede Stalin. This gave me the opportunity of taking up a vantage point close by the door Stalin was to come through. Just as I approached it, it was opened and I almost met Stalin head-on.

Out into the lounge stepped the "Father of the new Soviet Constitution," moving with slow and measured steps, and with what seemed to me a forced and granite-like smile on his face. But he was exuding obvious satisfaction over the cries of his name and the "Hurrahs!" which came from behind him.

Stalin turned his cold, steely eyes in my direction, and I felt as if I was being turned into a stone statue. They seemed to go through me like a high-speed bullet piercing a bull's-eye.

What did Stalin look like? How was he dressed? What were his physical features?

He was short and stocky and barrel-stomached. He was wearing a plain dark gray tunic, buttoned at the neck, with matching trousers going down into almost knee-high black boots. Under his somewhat curved nose was a walrus-like black mustache, topping a wide mouth. A few streaks of gray had begun to appear at the temples of his full head of black hair, brushed straight 'back from a receding forehead. His almond-shaped eyes attested to the dash of Mongolian blood in his ancestry.

It has become commonplace to refer to Stalin as a Russian, but he was not Russian by race. It is known that his father was a Georgian and his mother was an Ossetian, both members of Caucasus mountain tribes, though some sources claim the father was Ossetian and the mother Georgian. Either way, this accounted for his olive complexion and resemblance to Mediterranean races.

His face contained pockmarks, remnants of a bout with smallpox early in life. The defective, always bent left arm was shorter than the right and is said to have kept him from being mobilized into the Czarist Army.

After Stalin and his retinue had passed into the lounge, the delegates surged in. I was swept along with them as they followed him into the adjoining snow-white St. George's Hall, with its eighteen spiral columns and low-hanging massive chandeliers. Stalin all the while was seemingly reveling in this almost hysterical adulation.

I and many of my journalistic colleagues wrote favorably of the new charter in our dispatches. It seemed to us at least a start in the right direction.

Most of us had become very fond of the likable, open-hearted and hospitable Russian people; some of us had even married Russian girls. The hard-working Russian people, during the past seventeen years, had fully earned a greater measure of liberty than they hitherto had been given. We sincerely hoped the new constitution would become a functioning and living reality for them.

But we did not have long to wait for disillusionment—the Great Purges of 1938, soon separated us from our illusions.

CHAPTER X

A Chicagoan Disappears

Every man meets his Waterloo at last
—Wendell Phillips

ONE CASE DRAMATIZED FOR ME, as no other, the absoluteness of the purges. Lovett Forte-Whiteman was one of the early Negro pilgrims who journeyed to Moscow to worship at the "Kaaba" of Communism. Before his pilgrimage, Lovett Forte-Whiteman, who was a graduate of Tuskegee, had taken a leading role in organizing the American Negro Labor Congress in the mid-twenties. This forerunner of the National Negro Congress was short-lived and like some Negro intellectuals and "angry men" of the period, Lovett Forte-Whiteman broke with the Socialist Party and joined the American Communist Party. Leaving Chicago, he went to New York, and then to Russia. After reaching Moscow he decided to settle permanently in the country.

Lovett Forte-Whiteman was an affable person and after we met we often had long conversations. He told me he had also studied at the Armour Institute of Technology in Chicago and was currently doing fish-breeding research for the University of Moscow. Shortly after "coming home to Moscow," as he put it, he had married a Russian Jewish woman who was employed in a Moscow scientific research institution. They lived in a dank, dark room on Gazetny Peroulok, about half a block from the Central Telegraph Office on Tverskaya (now Gorky) Street.

He had adopted the practice of many Russian Communists of shaving his head, and with his sallow brown complexion and his finely-chiselled nose set into a V-shaped face he resembled a Buddhist monk, though I've been struck in recent months by his striking resemblance to the Black Muslim leader, Elijah Muhammad.

He was also a member of the Russian team that had written the scenario of the ill-fated *Black and White* film and had been a member of the Russian delegation which met and welcomed the American Negro group when they arrived in Leningrad in late June, 1932. Despite the fact that he had lived for several years in Russia and had close associations with Russians and a Russian-born wife, he had difficulty in speaking Russian intelligibly.

As a foreign Communist, Lovett Forte-Whiteman naturally had close connections with the Comintern and its allied organizations. He was often sent on speaking tours to Russian industrial and farming centers. On these tours he pleaded fervently for moral and material support for the Scottsboro Boys and Angelo Herndon, the Atlanta youth who had been sentenced to a Georgia chain gang for leading a thousand Negro and white families in a relief march on the capitol in Atlanta. He expounded loud and long on lynchings, Jim Crow and oppression of his people in America and condemned with fiery emotions the enslavement of black people in the African colonies of European imperialist nations.

These speaking tours never lasted long and Lovett Forte-Whiteman would be back in Moscow after a few days. But at other times, he disappeared from home for weeks at a time. All his wife would say was that "he has gone away on a komande-rovka (mission)." Where he had gone and why, she did not explain or perhaps did not know; nor could she say when he would return.

It was no secret in well-informed circles that the Comintern, like the foreign ministeries of most countries, used couriers to transport important documents and other highly-classified matter to and from other countries. It was possible, I surmised at the time, that Lovett Forte-Whiteman was acting as a Comintern courier during his lengthy absences.

He was always well-dressed in clothes of good quality and the sort of shoes that were unobtainable in Russia. Once when he returned from a long absence, I remarked that I admired his excellent clothes and shoes, adding that I should like to know here I could buy some for myself. He replied evasively and I asked no further questions.

Lovett Forte-Whiteman was steeped in Marxist ideology, dialectical materialism and the theory of the class struggle. He considered himself a leading theoretician on the Negro problem in the United States and the colonial question in Africa. He stoutly supported the Communist "line" of that time on a separate Negro state to be gerrymandered out of the southern American Black Belt. Incidentally, the "line" of the Black Muslims in America also propagates the establishment of a separate Black State.

This "thesis" of a separate Negro state struck me as being unrealistic, impracticable and segregation in reverse, I argued. How could the existing southern states be torn up to create a new Black State? What about the United States Constitution, Article IV, Section 3, which states specifically that "no new State shall be formed or erected within the Jurisdiction of any other State; nor any State be formed by Junction of two or more States, or Parts of States, without the consent of the Legislatures of the States concerned as well as of the Congress"?

Futhermore, I contended, the growing sentiment among America's Negro population was not for more separation,

but for more integration into the mainstream of American
life.

But Lovett Forte-Whiteman was a dyed-in-the-wool Communist dogmatist; for him there could be no deviation from
the accepted Communist "line." Any deviation invited trouble,
and if persisted in, expulsion from the elite ranks of the Communist Party.

"You are a political ignoramus," he retorted. "After the proletarian revolution in America, we Communists will have control. We will create the Black State."

There was a small group of American Negroes living in
Russia at that time. Practically all of them belonged in the
category of intellectuals—that is, most of them had been college educated. While they were all interested in what was going on in Russia—the building of a new form of society—
they were classified as "non-politicals" and distinct from other
Negroes, mainly from Africa and the West Indies, who
were being trained as revolutionaries in Communist political
schools.

Lovett Forte-Whiteman considered himself the mentor of
this group and did his best to proselytize and indoctrinate
them. He often invited them, singly or in groups, to have lunch
with him and unfailingly he channeled the conversation
around to political subjects. His Negro guests relished the food
and drinks, but the indoctrination dish did not prove as digest-
ible. The theoretical, dogmatic Marxist explanations of the
class struggle and the inevitability of the coming proletarian
revolution or the contention that the Negro was a powerful reserve in the revolutionary struggle was just too much for his
guests to swallow.

The unmistakable obstacle was that though this group was
roughly leftist oriented, they came from different social back-
grounds. Some came from comfortable middle class, professional families, others better-than-average wage-earning or
farm-owning families. They simply did not have any coherent

proletarian background. While they were all colored, they represented disparate social groupings. Their ambitions were not proletarian; they desired to rise in the social scale.

At about this time, Lovett Forte-Whiteman committed what, in my opinion, was the greatest *faux pas* of all. He advised and insisted—perhaps for some Communist Dialectical reason—that the group should maintain a high degree of consciousness of their color and always remember that they were Negroes. But the complete absence of any racial prejudice or discrimination and the almost total lack of color consciousness in Russia made Lovett Forte-Whiteman's advice extremely unpalatable. It was a blunder which was particularly irritating and unacceptable.

As a matter of fact, a Negro in Russia had no reason at all to think of color. Most not only wanted to, but were fast forgetting about their color, escaping if you will. One of Lovett Forte-Whiteman's guests called him a "Red racist," another chimed in with "Communist Uncle Tom" and a third asked him why he didn't go to Mississippi if he approved of "going around with a black chip on his shoulder?"

Lovett Forte-Whiteman often referred to his friends whose names were in the Communist "Who's Who," such important Bolsheviks as Bukharin, Radek, Tomsky, Rykov, Kamenev, Litvinov, Zinoviev and several other lesser lights of the Communist elite. Bukharin, Rykov, Kamenev and Zinoviev were later executed; Radek was sent to a concentration camp; and Tomsky committed suicide. He was a great admirer of Lenin and Trotsky and confided to me privately that he felt the present Stalinist rule was becoming more and more deviationist— that is, was leading the revolution away from, and betraying the basic ideals and aims of, Marxism and Leninism.

He asked me one day if I would like to meet Nikolai Bukharin and Karl Radek, then the leading figures in Moscow journalism. He said he could easily arrange it, but I said that I had no particular desire to meet these Bolshevik newsmen

whose journalism was so very different from mine. He dropped
the subject and never raised it again.

One day I raised the question of why, since he knew all
those powerful Communist figures, he did not obtain better,
more spacious living quarters?

"We Communists like to live modestly and selflessly," he
answered. "Within a few years there will be an abundance of
housing and comfort for all."

But despite this prediction, when I left Russia a decade
later, the housing situation was still very acute, and even today,
in 1964, reports coming out of Russia indicate a continuing
severe housing shortage.

During my years in Moscow there appeared in the foreign
press many reports of Moscow gold being sent to the outside
world for fomenting and financing revolutionary organizations and movements. I asked Lovett Forte-Whiteman what he
thought of these reports. His answer was revealing of the man's
devotion to Communism and its ideals and aims.

"And why not? Why should not financial assistance be
provided to fraternal parties and progressive movements to
break the yoke of capitalist exploitation and colonial enslavement?

"Furthermore, it is no secret to us Communists that capitalist and imperialist governments and even big business supply
money and guns for the undermining and overthrow of governments in small, weak countries that operate contrary to their
policies and interests."

One foreign source implied that this Moscow gold was
reaching foreign countries in money belts worn by special,
trusted couriers. I recalled that Lovett Forte-Whiteman once
told me he had visited some of the countries mentioned, in
the Middle and Near East, as well as Europe. And while he
had not explained the purpose of these missions—and I had
not pressed him for an explanation—I did recall his regular
and prolonged absences from Moscow. It occurred to me again

that he might have been serving as a courier in the transporting of funds.

About a year after the beginning of the great Moscow purge trials in 1936, Lovett Forte-Whiteman disappeared. One day I called at his home. There was no answer to my first knocks, but I persisted. Finally, Mrs. Lovett Forte-Whiteman cracked the door open.

"Is Gospodin Forte-Whiteman at home?" I asked.

"No, he isn't, and I beg you never to come here looking for him again," she replied tartly.

I had been living in Russia long enough to understand the implications. The broom had been sweeping steadily since the purge trials began. I had been attending the trials of the high-ranking victims in a small hall in the House of the Unions (former Club of the Nobility); but thousands of lesser victims, I knew, simply disappeared or were liquidated without benefit of trial.

It seems certain to me that Lovett Forte-Whiteman was swept up along with other lesser victims of the terror. What his "crime" had been may never be known, but bits of information reaching me from different sources afterwards indicated that he had died in a concentration camp about two years after his disappearance.

I, of course, had no means of confirming this information, but I do know that he was never seen again.

CHAPTER XI

The Russian Press:
Some Observations

Citizens of the USSR are guaranteed by law (b) freedom of the press.
—Chapter 10, Article 125, Soviet Constitution

B E GOOD ENOUGH to write us an article about the condition of the Negro people in the United States."

This request was made to me by the editor of a Russian publication in the mid-thirties. I got busy and within ten days I
delivered a three thousand word article to him. I suggested
that I should like to see my article published "as is" an *in toto.*
The piece was never published, though I was paid one thous-
and rubles (all kinds of writing was well paid for in Russia)
for it. Why was the article never published?

The reason, I suspected, was that I had made the mistake of
writing a balanced article, showing both the dark and bright
sides of Negro life in America. What was wanted, no doubt,
was only the dark side—which would have made a far more
effective propaganda impact on Russian readers, especially on
Soviet minority peoples, who were being assured that they
were better off in all respects than any other minority group
in the world. (I make no attempt to deny that the Soviet system has brought appreciable material benefits to most of the
country's minority peoples.)

It was my conjecture that it was not the editor who made the final decision against publishing the article. He had had to submit it for final approval to GLAVLIT (Central Administration of Literature and Publishing) and no doubt they had not approved it. GLAVLIT was the inescapable and final arbiter of everything published in Russia. If GLAVLIT's censors said "Nyet," that was that; there was no reconsideration.

Even such an innocuous publication as a dictionary had to be approved by GLAVLIT. For example, I purchased an English-Russian and a Russian-English dictionary which had been compiled by Professors V. K. Muller and S. K. Boyanus and published by the State Publishing Institute "Soviet Encyclopaedia" in 1937. These were the finest dictionaries of these two languages ever published; together they contained one hundred twenty thousand words. And right there in small type at the bottom of the title page I read: GLAVLIT A568. This was GLAVLIT's imprimatur.

GLAVLIT was established by a decree of the Soviet Government in 1921 for "maintaining the strictest politico-ideological control over printed matter, manuscripts, photographs, paintings, cartoons, etc." This control organization remained, notwithstanding the "guarantee" of freedom of the press in the Soviet Constitution, as the supreme censor of everything printed and published in Russia.

GLAVLIT's censors sat in judgment in every publishing house and printing plant, and not one copy of any newspaper, magazine, book, pamphlet, leaflet, dictionary, cookbook, or even the telephone directory could be run through the presses and released to the public without its OK. I understand that GLAVLIT is still functioning, though perhaps with less arbitrariness than in former years.

This supreme censorship organization's tentacles even reached into the Academy of Science's printing and publishing activities. For in their theoretical and practical work, scientists "must be guided by the spirit of the Bolshevik Party approach," according to an article by A. P. Topshiyev appearing in *Pravda* in August of 1949. If the venerable scientists were not so oriented, it was GLAVLIT's duty to see that no non-Bolshevik slant ever got into print.

I got the impression that this pre-publication censorship did have some advantages for Soviet writers; they could not go wrong in print, thereby avoiding subjecting themselves to the wrath of the regime. Editors and editorial writers had comparatively easy jobs. The party line and government policy at any given time readily provided pegs for editorials and leads for feature stories; hence, the creative and critical faculties played little or nor part in the editorial process. Yet Soviet press workers had to possess great flexibility—quick switches had to be made if the official "line" changed, as it often did.

Prior to World War II, for example, the Soviet Press was sharply anti-Nazi and anti-Fascist. So were the Soviet people. However, after the signing of the Hitler-Stalin Pact in 1939, the press suddenly became friendly toward Germany and Italy and antagonistic toward England, France and Poland. The European countries that had been attacked by Hitler Germany were accused in the Soviet Press of having attacked Germany! Yet, in 1954, a leading Soviet publication was to write that Germany, Japan and Italy "set out to solve their problems by armed aggression and war. . . . It was this aggressive alliance which unleashed World War II by attacking the European countries in 1939, and the United States two years later." (*New Times*, No. 20, 1954.)

After the signing of the Hitler-Stalin Pact, German newspaper correspondents made their appearance in Moscow and were warmly welcomed. Soviet newspapers played up conspicuously war news of German land victories and destructive air raids on England. This war news originated in Berlin and most of it was published with the credit-line of DNB (German News Bureau).

Ever since the Communists took over rule of Russia in

1917, they have never wavered in believing that the press is a powerful weapon. And this led me to believe that that was the main reason why freedom of the press was denied to the people—it might prove to be a powerful weapon for them too.

American Negroes will readily admit that the Negro Press has been a powerful weapon in their struggle for full civil rights and the eradication of second-class citizenship in the United States. Soviet minority peoples had no such unrestricted weapon at their disposal, Soviet constitutional "guarantees" to the contrary notwithstanding. No attempt is made here to claim that Soviet minorities were subjected to second class citizenship; but they did have certain peculiar social, religious and linguistic problems that were being encroached upon and that a genuine "free press" could have defended.

The American Negro Press, and the press of any other minority people in the United States, can openly and sharply criticize any department and any official, high or low, of the Federal, State or Local governments. And such criticism cannot be silenced. If, hypothetically, the Congress should pass a law aimed at restricting the freedom of the press, the United States Supreme Court would declare such legislation null and void and in direct violation of an Amendment to the Constitution, which forbids "abridging the freedom of the press."

Incidentally, I recall discussing the American Negro Press with an important young Russian journalist one evening at the Journalists' Club. When I told him that there were some two hundred Negro newspapers in the United States, with some of the larger having their own, self-contained printing plants, he asked, "Can Negroes operate the presses, linotypes and other mechanical equipment?" No, he was wholly innocent of attempting to downgrade Negro skills; he was just completely ignorant of reality in America.

Pravda, organ of the Communist Party of the Soviet Union, was, and is, the leading, most authoritative and definitive newspaper in Russia. *Pravda* means "Truth" in Russian, and if

Russians say they saw it in *Pravda,* then it had to be true whether they liked it or agreed with it. Whatever appeared in this newspaper was the editorial peg for all the seven thousand newspapers and nine hundred and sixty magazines being published when I left Russia after the end of World War II. Woe to any editor who attempted to deviate from the "line" laid down by *Pravda.*

None of these thousands of publications was "owned," as far as I could make out, by the people. The people did not appear to have any voice in selecting or appointing editors, all of whom, whether Communist Party members or not, had to be "cleared" and approved by the Party. "One of the first obligations of Party leadership is to select newspaper workers meticulously, especially to make a strict approach to the choice of candidates for editorships." (*Leningrad Pravda,* Communist Party organ, May 26, 1950.)

I was unable to find that reader interest had any meaning for editors or any bearing on news policy for newspapers and magazines. There were no crusading editors speaking out boldly and fearlessly against obvious injustices or denouncing unpopular governmental measures. There were, it is true, "crusading" editors, but they all "crusaded" for the Party "line." "The newspapers are destined to play a leading role in the Communist training of people, in the propagation of the ideas of Marxism-Leninism." (*Pravda,* October 18, 1946.)

During my years of residence in Russia, I never saw a foreign newspaper or magazine on sale at a newsstand or in a bookshop. Of course, foreign Communist newspapers and other publications always were on sale at *Mezhdurodnaya Kniga* (International Bookshop) on Kuznetsky Most, the government organization which controlled the import and export of all publications entering and leaving the country. This I took to mean that the Russian people were being denied the freedom of buying and reading foreign newspapers and magazines, though I knew many Russians who were eager to do so.

This is not to say that no foreign newspapers and magazines were reaching Russia. They were, but they were not available to the general public. American and European scientific and technical publications were reaching Soviet scientific and research institutions, where they were avidly read and thoroughly combed by Soviet scientists and engineers.

I once heard that thirty-six copies of the *New York Times* reached Moscow by subscription. But these copies were kept under lock and key in "closed" libraries—that is, libraries to which access was granted to only a restricted number of persons.

And I learned that sometimes there were libraries within libraries. While the general sections of most libraries were accessible to the general public, entry into so-called "special fund" departments containing foreign publications was limited to only the most trusted and "uncontaminable" persons. In these inner sanctums could be found a varied selection of Western bourgeois newspapers and magazines.

Such publications, I assumed, were not for ordinary readers' eyes because they contained too many of the advantages of life in the bourgeois world—including big display advertisements of plentiful goods at comparatively cheap prices. Such publications contained too much "bourgeois poison," too many "slanders" against the Soviet Union. Such reading matter might prove "contaminating" to ordinary Soviet people.

A Russian friend of mine had a relative in New York subscribe to several American newspapers and magazines, giving the name and mailing address of his Moscow relative. The publications were duly mailed, but the addressee received none of them. And out of fear, he never inquired at the post office why he had not.

One small concession permitting Russians to read foreign-edited publications was grudgingly made during the war. The British Government was permitted to publish the *British Ally* and the United States Government was allowed to distribute the slick, typographically-excellent magazine *Amerika,* both printed in Russian. There was a great demand for these publications and they were eagerly read by the Soviet citizens who managed to obtain copies.

Incidentally, I had a regular "route" for *Amerika.* The American Embassy supplied me with twelve copies and these I passed along to neighbors in the apartment house where I lived. But usually I reached home with only five or six copies.

On the autobus or trolleybus I used to open and thumb through a copy and ogling passengers next to me whispered, "Skolko stoit?" (What's the price?). I gave them copies free of charge, keeping a few for my regular neighbor "customers." I often saw these a few days later—already dogs-eared.

It has always been my opinion that American and British wire services or large newspapers which maintained bureaus in Russia were willy-nilly rendering a valuable, free service to the Soviet Government. These agencies and newspapers were devoting large sums of money toward spreading before foreign readers only what the Soviet authorities wanted them to read.

In practice, the reading fare of foreign readers was being regulated and controlled, inasmuch as nothing could be cabled "out" to the foreign press except what had been approved. Unless it met the approval of the Soviet censors, it just was not permitted to be cabled abroad.

Old Russia-hands, anxious to get their stories through, performed careful pre-censoring on their stories before submitting them to the censors. This had its advantages from an operational standpoint: it prevented unnecessary wrangling with the censors and prevented cables from being unduly delayed or even "killed." I know of cases where cables which had not been adequately pre-censored by the writers were so emaciated by the censors that they were unintelligible to foreign cable editors when they arrived.

Actually, many of the censors were not too well acquainted with the nuances of the English language. There often occurred hair-splitting wrangles over the meaning of words. As a typical example, one of my cables explaining the reactions of the Russian people to the death of President Roosevelt referred to the "late, lamented President." The censor held up the cable, and when I demanded to know why he "explained" that he could not pass a cable which called Roosevelt a "lame" President. Another correspondent once referred in a cable to Stalin as the "Fuehrer of the Soviet Union," and no explanation could convince the censor that "Leader of the Soviet Union," meant exactly the same thing.

Foreign correspondents' cables are not now being censored. But this can have its disadvantages, too. While it undoubtedly provides quicker transmission, the correspondents must always remain uneasy about the after effect. When cables are censored and passed, correspondents could feel that their resident permits were "safe."

Soviet censorship, I observed, was like Janus: it "watched" two ways—it prevented any "undesirable" news being cabled out of the country and it prevented any "undesirable" news from reaching Soviet readers. This combination created an unbreachable news *cordon sanitaire.*

I recall having discussed with some of my Russian friends the guarantee of freedom of the press as a "fundamental right" of Soviet citizens embedded in their constitution. Some of my less naïve friends admitted that it was impossible for Soviet citizens to make use of this "guarantee" and "fundamental right."

All printing plants and paper mills, ink and paper supplies in Russia were under the strict and exclusive administration of the Communist Party and/or the Soviet Government. All such facilities were closely guarded day and night by armed guards. No working class man or woman could enter any printing plant or paper warehouse without special permission; even people working in such places had to carry passes bearing their photographs.

The press as I knew it in Russia certainly enjoyed far less freedom than the Russian Press had enjoyed under Czarism, as many of my older Russian friends confirmed. But perhaps in the new Communist lexicon the word "freedom" has assumed a different meaning.

CHAPTER XII

The End of the Beginning

"When detected lying, they did not blush,
but answered reproofs with a sneer."
— Vladimir Klyuchevsky on 17th Century
Russian diplomacy

IT WAS ONE OF THOSE LONG winter nights in northern Russia
when darkness begins falling at four o'clock in the afternoon. A biting cold wind, sweeping down from the Ural
Mountains out of Siberia, was adding to the frigidity of winter's grip on Moscow. Such weather can be experienced in the
United States only in Minnesota, North Dakota and Montana.

I was disturbed from my re-reading of Gogol's *Dead Souls*
by the telephone ringing in my hotel room. The caller was one
of my journalistic colleagues with an appealing invitation
that promised to eliminate some of the dreariness from the
night.

"One of my girl friends just called and said she and a pretty
friend are very lonesome tonight," my caller said. "What about
a night out with them? Come along!"

On such a night the proposal seemed very intriguing. What
could be more pleasant than spending a long winter evening
with two charming and busty Russian girls over caviar and
Crimean wine in a snug corner of some secluded cafe?

Our rendezvous was to be on Pushkin Square at seven o'clock. And at ten minutes before the appointed hour, snug in my fur-lined overcoat and with my brown mink fur cap resting at a jaunty angle on my head, I was on my way.

Although my colleague and I had lived for several years in Russia, where being on time was universally ignored, we had not lost our western custom of arriving for appointments on time. And as the Kremlin clock boomed out seven times in the distance, we met on the broad and icy square.

The fact that the girls were not there was understandable to us: they were Russian and Russians were notorious for always being late. Furthermore, Moscow's transport system was very undependable and I knew that they might have been delayed waiting for a bus or tramcar.

Standing immobile in such wintry weather is not recommended, so we began pacing back and forth across the murky square.

"Oh, don't worry, they'll be coming," my companion assured me at eight o'clock.

Fifteen minutes earlier I had noticed two husky men in black overcoats and black fur caps pacing back and forth across the square. When we turned at one side of the square, they turned at the opposite side, usually passing us in the center. But I gave no thought to this; perhaps their "dates" were late, too.

But as we were making our crossing just after eight o'clock, instead of by-passing us as they had been doing previously, they met us head-on. Tapping us on the shoulder, they said, "Come along with us."

"What for? Who are you?" I asked.

"Never mind, don't try to resist authority."

I noticed that my colleague uttered not one word of protest, the reason for which I shall later offer a reasonable surmise.

The men in black escorted us through a courtyard and into the ground floor of an old building on nearby Bolshaya Bronnaya Ulitsa. I was directed into one room, my companion into another.

After another man in uniform, who appeared to be an officer, came into the room, I was politely asked to take off my overcoat and jacket, shoes and cap. After asking me to sit down, they went to work.

The linings of my overcoat, jacket and fur cap were ripped open with a razor blade. Deft hands examined the space inside each. The soles and heels and inner soles of my boots were then thoroughly examined. I was asked to stand up and was carefully frisked. I assumed that the same thing was being performed on my colleague in another room.

I suffered this ordeal with complete equanimity, since I was convinced that I had nothing incriminating in my clothes or on my person. But, as a precaution, I watched every move very attentively to make certain that no incriminatory "plant" was "found" in my clothes. My only apprehension was that I might be subjected to a third degree.

"You may dress and go now," the officer said. "Excuse us for having disturbed you."

As I looked over my ripped clothes, I asked what they intended doing about the linings.

"Oh, that's a small matter," the officer answered. "You can find a tailor to sew the linings back."

As I emerged into the outer room buttoning up my overcoat, my colleague came out of another room, to all appearances undishevelled.

"What happened?" I asked as we passed out into the bitter cold.

"Nothing much," he answered. "They merely told me not to talk."

Now my journalistic colleague, he who had invited me to join him in a pleasant winter evening with two lovely Russian girls, was Moscow correspondent for a foreign Communist newspaper. Was the "date" merely a trick to make my interception easy?

To this day I still feel that there was something smacking strongly of deceit in the whole affair—with my colleague acting as middleman.

When I went next day to a tailor, the old man seemed quite unconcerned over the condition of my clothes. "It looks as if you have fallen into the hands of the Black Ravens," he remarked, eyeing me and winking understandingly over his glasses. Russians themselves referred to their Secret Police Agents as Black Ravens.

But though nothing had really come of my brush with the MVD, it was for me somehow the end of the beginning. It actually went back farther than this, however, probably to the time when I had left the Postal Service to devote my full time of journalism. Actually, that had not been my sole reason for not renewing my contract. My utter disillusionment with the prevailing fear and terror had begun with the assassination of top-ranking Leningrad party boss, Sergei Kirov in party headquarters. It really hit home, however, when my boss, Postmaster Uvarov was liquidated along with several other postal officials that I knew personally. Many disappeared without a trace. Postal employees had begun talking in whispers and looking back over their shoulders. Stalin's Secret Police had begun to show a keen interest in the Postal Service.

This jungle of terror was not for me, I decided, so when my contract expired in 1935 I did not renew it. Instead I cast my lot with news reporting. Besides it was in that year that I first met Marie Petrovna, though I was not to see her again until two years later.

CHAPTER XIII

Marie Petrovna

Beauty is altogether in the eye of the beholder.
—Lew Wallace

IT HAD BEEN ON NEW YEAR'S EVE. Christmas had come and gone; it had meant nothing more to atheistic Russia than just another date on the calendar. But one of the biggest and most festive non-political holidays—if anything can be called non-political in Russia—was and still is the celebration of the arrival of the New Year.

A giant fir tree—just like a Christmas tree anywhere, but without any Yuletide connotations—had been placed in the center of the spacious, lofty, snow-white hall of the former Club of the Nobility, just off Red Square. Thousands of young Russians were gathering here to greet the New Year with a students' ball. Now, these New Year students balls are held in the Kremlin, but in the period I am writing about the Kremlin was as inaccessible to ordinary Russians as the former Turkish Sultan's harem was to Turkish playboys.

A schoolteacher friend of mine had invited me to accompany her to the celebration. We occupied seats in a loge behind the balustrade on the main floor to watch the students dance and sing around the New Year's tree, holding long colored streamers, rather like a Maypole celebration in America.

One young brunette girl whirled close to our loge, holding her streamer and skipping with youthful abandon. Russians are overwhelmingly a blond race, with brunettes a rarity, thereby making them stand out conspicuously in any gathering.

"Who is that rosy-faced brunette?" I asked.

"Oh, that's Marie Petrovna, one of our Moscow beauties. Isn't she lovely?" My companion replied, "Would you like to meet her?"

So during an intermission in the merrymaking, my companion beckoned the girl over to our loge.

"Marie Petrovna, meet my American friend."

"How pleasant," Marie Petrovna answered, curtsying. When being introduced in Russia, it is customary for the person to whom one has been presented to reply, "Kak priyartno" (How pleasant) or just "Priyartno" (Pleasant).

Just then the music started up again and Marie Petrovna was off to grab a streamer and resume her dancing, but every time she swept past our loge, usually giving us a smile, my eyes followed her like a theater spotlight focusing on a stage star. I thought she was the most beautiful girl I had ever seen and thought idly of Natalya Goncharova, the Moscow beauty that Pushkin had married.

The ball ended in the early morning hours and the young merrymakers scattered for home in the bitter cold. Now, Moscow is a vast city and I did not know Marie Petrovna's address, so I wondered if I would ever see her again. But I made a firm decision: I must somehow, somewhere, see her again, even though I had to wait a long time.

Time passed—1935, 1936, 1937. I was waiting; I still had plenty of patience. I went to the New Year's Eve student ball each year but Marie Petrovna did not attend.

Then on Christmas evening (only a date on the calendar) in 1937, with nothing much to do, I decided to go to the Journalist's Club, to which I had a guest membership, where a film with Deanna Durbin called *100 Men And A Girl* was being shown.

I arrived after the showing had begun, but an usher found me a seat in the front row of the darkened hall. When the lights came on, I turned to my left and there, sitting next to me, was Marie Petrovna. My heart began pounding as she looked my way.

"Hello!" I said. "Do you remember me?"

"Of course I do," she replied.

"You have grown up since I saw you last," I remarked.

She was with another Russian girl and two young gentlemen friends. After the film ended everybody was going to the restaurant downstairs, and Marie Petrovna invited me to join her party.

There was music and dancing in the restaurant and once when the other members of our party were dancing, Marie Petrovna and I decided to sit this one out. This gave us an opportunity to become better acquainted and we exchanged addresses and telephone numbers. What is more, we made an appointment to meet at the Alexander Pushkin statue on Pushkin Square the following evening.

There was one unusual thing that I soon discovered about Marie Petrovna. She had been born in 1918, four months after the Communist Revolution had overthrown the Provisional Government, and had grown up under Communist rule, without ever experiencing any other form of government in her country. Yet she was one of the most apolitical young Russians I had ever met. She had never joined the Octobrists or Pioneers (Communist organizations for children), nor did she have any intention of joining the Komsomols, another Communist organization for young Russians.

Marie Petrovna was just not interested in politics of any

kind and, like her parents, she had remained deeply religious despite the fact that all the churches had been closed. One can, of course, be religious without going to church every Sunday.

Although Marxism-Leninism-Stalinism had penetrated into music, literature, painting, the theater and every other facet of Soviet society, the eternal human emotion of love seems impermeable to political ideology. Love and courtship in Russia follows the same general pattern as in capitalist America— boy meets girls, they like each other, they begin "going steady," love develops and eventually they marry.

But in between these stages, there were "operational" problems that do not exist in America. There were no family cars to park in romantic spots, since Russian families just didn't have cars. And private love-making at home was all but impossible as almost all Russian families lived in one or at most two rooms. Actually, Marie Petrovna's family had two.

The benches along the Moscow River embankment by the Kremlin wall and those spotting the long and shady boulevards were ideal places on white summer nights for romance. Also there were excursion boats plying back and forth on the Moscow-Volga Canal and numerous secluded spots in the vast Park of Culture and Rest and in Sokolniky Park, where Vice President Nixon and Premier Nikita Khrushchev had their famous wrangle during the American Exhibition in 1959.

In wintertime, Marie Petrovna and I were regular habitués of the Bolshoi and other theaters in Moscow—excellent places for holding hands. And we were also regular skating partners at the city's numerous rinks.

Russian girls are so independent that they do not have to ask parental consent to marry; it would have been considered puritanically bourgeois for a young man, sheepishly and hesitatingly, to ask a father for the hand of his daughter. Parents were merely informed of a *fait accompli*. And that's just what Marie Petrovna did after we went to the Marriage Bureau and

signed our names in the Registry in January of 1938. Later, at
a simple family dinner at her home, her father hugged me and
exclaimed, "My dear son-in-law, you have taken my beauty
away from me."

Our marriage was later to give Marie Petrovna her first opportunity for moving in high bourgeois society. The names of
foreign correspondents were in the invitation lists of all the
foreign diplomatic missions in Moscow. There were continual
rounds of cocktail parties and receptions marking the national
days of different countries.

The gracious manners of foreign society were detested by
the regime. The teaching of western etiquette to children was
considered unpardonable kowtowing to trivial and decadent
bourgeois deportment and customs. The wearing of neckties,
pressed pants, hats and polished shoes was considered un-pro-
letarian. Women wore any dresses they had—even to the opera
in the gilded Bolshoi Theater. And these dresses usually were
plain cotton cloth and not ironed. Unkemptness, slovenliness
and looking like a beatnik were the accepted rules and marks
of the true proletarian.

Being a guest at bourgeois affairs was new and strange for
Marie Petrovna. She had been born and raised in a proletarian
society. I had to coach her in the practices and manners of
western society. She responded splendidly, and after her few
first contacts she accommodated herself to this new milieu with
ease and grace.

A private seamstress made her neat and correct clothes without any frills. These plain though appropriate clothes seemed
to add to her attractiveness. After arriving at these affairs, I
was able to spend little time with her. She was always surrounded by attentive male guests. Foreign women guests admired her fresh and rosy-cheeked Russian beauty.

Every week invitations came requesting the company of
"Monsieur Homer Smith and Madame." At the French Embassy we were introduced to the towering and austere General

Charles De Gaulle. The Chinese turned on their Oriental charm at the Chinese Embassy. At the Mexican Embassy, Latin warmth prevailed. The charming wife of the Ethiopian Minister and Marie Petrovna were inseparable companions. Marie Petrovna curtsied with consummate grace before the gorgeous and ravishing sister of the Shah of Persia, Princess Ashraf, at the Persian Embassy.

In his book, *My Three Years In Moscow,* Walter Bedell Smith, American Ambassador to Russia, mentioned the flea incident at the Persian Embassy. Marie Petrovna and I witnessed that incident. We arrived at the Embassy in the Associated Press car immediately behind Ambassador Smith's car. We arrived late, and this placed us at the end of the line of guests moving slowly pass the Princess.

European guests ahead of us were being introduced to peach-colored and smiling Princess Ashraf. The men were kissing her slender and bejewelled hand. Her white satin gown, black hair and large dark eyes and emerald earrings hanging low, and her classical features—all these made her look like a goddess plucked from the side of a Persian urn.

Ambassador Smith, turning and in an aside to me, remarked:

"Homer, are you ready? We can't let those Europeans have better manners than us."

When our turn came, we duly took the Princess' soft and perfumed hand and deftly planted American kisses on it. Afterward, Ambassador Smith remarked jocundly:

"Homer, you know one thing. That woman is so lovely that a man would be ready to kiss her feet."

After the hand-kissing formalities had ended, Ambassador Smith found his way back to the Princess for a chat. She suggested sitting on a divan. Marie Patrovna and I watched from the sidelines. Suddenly, I noticed Princess Ashraf make a sharp jerk. A flea apparently had crawled out of a seam on the back of the divan, reached the Princess' bare back and tasted Royal Persian blood.

At another diplomatic party in the National Hotel one autumn night near the end of the war, I was unable to find a taxicab to take us home. Seeing our predicament, the Mexican Ambassador, Señor Luis Quintanilla, who was a good friend of ours, offered his car. He and his American wife went along for the ride to our house.

The war-time blackout and curfew were still in effect, though less rigid than it had been earlier in the war. We headed up Gorky Street, past the Byelorussian Railway Station and continued out Leningrad Chaussee. Suddenly, two policemen stepped out of the darkness onto the roadway. One stood in front of the car, the other beamed his flashlight into the car.

Ambassador Quintanilla and his wife spoke no Russian. The Russian chauffeur and I got out of the car and began remonstrating with the policemen. I told them to begone, that this was a diplomatic car.

But the looks of the car and its passengers did not support my contention. The war had prevented new cars from reaching Russia, and the Mexican Ambassador had managed to wheedle an old and decrepit Ford car out of the Soviet Government. The policemen were clearly and justifiably in doubt about this old rattle-trap being a diplomatic vehicle. Adding to their doubt were the assorted passengers. The Ambassador looked exactly like an Aztec Indian; I looked like what I was. The night was still—the Mexican flag hung limp from its staff on the front left fender of the car. I moved to the front of the car and held the flag open. One of the policemen turned his flashlight on it—there was the figure of a large eagle in the white center stripe doing battle with a squirming snake. The policemen appeared baffled; they had never seen such a strange flag. But this appeared to convince them that this was in fact some sort of diplomatic vehicle. They relented, saluted and waved us on.

The longest and most sumptuous affair that Marie Petrovna

and I ever attended was the Victory Ball given by the Soviet Government to mark the surrender of Germany. This affair was given in the luxurious official Spiridonovsky Guest House, former mansion of a Russian merchant prince. One could get lost in this spacious two-story mansion; back of it was a lovely flower garden with walks and benches.

The affair began at nine o'clock of a white night summer evening. The entire foreign Diplomatic Corps was present. Foreign military officers stationed in Russia, Russian Marshals and Generals heavily bedecked with medals turned out in dress uniforms. Stars of the Russian theatrical world performed for the guests. There was music and dancing. Barrels of vodka and tubs of caviar must have been consumed that night.

It was broad daylight when the affair ended the next morning. Looking out into the flower garden, I saw three men stretched out on benches. Whether they were Russians or foreigners I did not know. I myself felt like going out and joining them to cool off. I might have done so had Marie Petrovna not been with me. That was the party that was. Of course, the Russians always did things of this sort in a big way.

Then our troubles began. The times were inauspicious for a foreigner to become a member of a Russian family. The bloody purges were still on and all foreigners, white or black, were suspected of engaging in espionage. Marie soon lost her job and could not find another. Every application blank that she filled in had to show the name Smith—and that obviously was a foreign name. She and her parents came under Secret Police surveillance because a foreigner was now a member of the family—even though they, and he, were honest people not engaged in any sort of illegal activity. It was not my color, for a change. In Moscow, my nationality was quite enough.

Inwardly, I strengthened my resolve to leave Russia. I had begun to question the intelligence of remaining even before leaving the Postal Service. My disappointment had grown with the passing years. Downright fear of the Secret Police was universal. No one who wished to sleep through the coming night dared to criticize the bad conditions under which he lived. This did not directly affect me, but nonetheless I suffered mental anguish because of it.

As always, I traded in well stocked shops where only valuta (foreign money) was accepted. These shops were out of bounds for the Russian citizen. I received my clothes from home because Russian clothes were made of such low quality and so poorly tailored. Besides, a suit cost about one thousand rubles, which is two hundred dollars in American money. I, as a foreign newsman, fared well enough, but other Negroes who had come to Russia seeking a better life had been less successful.

My direct contacts with these expatriates convinced me that they would certainly have been better off materially in the United States. They had all, long since, worn out their good American clothing and now were living, on their subsistence salaries, a step above starvation. They had equality to be sure, but there was also a poverty line which they shared equally with the Russians. I often mulled over the questions posed by this; was the racial equality worth the bare subsistence living in an atmosphere filled with fear and suspicion? I believe that every Negro who lived in Russia was primarily interested in the complete racial equality that existed there, but was this enough compensation for the lack of material amenities and the absence of civil liberties?

I cannot speak for all Negroes, but for me it was not. But after 1938, international events were moving in such a chaotic manner that it was nearly impossible for me to make any definitive plans for leaving Russia with my wife.

Political agreements, as well as economic and trade agreements between Russia and Germany, culminating in the notorius Molotov-Ribbentrop Pact, were signed in Moscow during August of 1939. The political agreements were openly publicized, but attached to the Pact was a secret pact within a pact, dividing Poland and the Baltic States between Russia and Germany and assigning Russia a sphere of influence in the direction of India and the Persian Gulf. Though we didn't know it then, this was the appetizer in the menu labeled World War II.

The Soviet people knew even less about what was happening than the outside world. The shift in diplomacy caught even the most professional observers off guard. Many were relieved at the seemingly relaxation of the threat of a Russian-German conflict, but the signing of the three-power Axis pact (Germany, Italy and Japan) in September, 1940, strained the newly tied bonds. This was the situation as June, 1941, approached.

CHAPTER XIV

The Siege of Moscow

I express the warmest congratulations of the Soviet Government on the splendid success of German arms.
—Molotov, June 18, 1940, complimenting Hitler's crushing of France and Norway.

EARLY IN THE MORNING of June 22, 1941, Soviet Foreign Minister Vyacheslav Molotov announced over the Moscow radio that Germany had attacked Russia.

Three hours earlier German Foreign Minister Joachim von Ribbentrop had delivered the formal declaration of war to the Soviet Ambassador in Berlin and two hours before that the German Ambassador in Moscow, Count Schulenberg, had read the declaration to Molotov in the Kremlin.

"It is war," Molotov observed, adding that German aircraft had been reported already bombing Russian towns and villages.

Even as I listened to the radio, Hitler's Wehrmacht was pouring into Russia from Poland with 168 superb divisions. Spearheading toward Moscow was the Central Army Group of 50 divisions under von Bock; 41 Southern Army Group divisions under von Rundstedt were driving across southern Russia; and 29 divisions of the Northern Army Group under von Leeb had Leningrad as its first target. Other divisions were on the move elsewhere, supposedly op-

erating with the Finns in the north and Rumanians in the
south.

All during that morning, from my window, I could see
knots of people in the street talking agitatedly. I decided to go
downtown for the latest newspapers and official communiqués,
but hardly had I passed out of the courtyard before I noticed a
militiaman (policeman) headed in my direction.

"Dokument!" he demanded.

I handed him my foreign correspondent's press card. He
perused it, handed it back, saluted and moved on. This had
never happened to me before in my neighborhood and I presumed that it was an early outcropping of the war hysteria
which would mount the nearer the Germans approached
Moscow.

My streetcar did not go directly downtown, and I had to
change to a trolleybus at the Byelorussian Railway Station.
While waiting for it, I met an old friend. As we chatted he told
me he had moved, and gave me his new address and telephone
number. Not wanting to forget his new address and telephone
number, I took my notebook out of my brief case to jot them
down after he had gone and as I was doing so, a woman pushing a wheelbarrow passed. I noticed that she was watching me
closely out of the corners of her eyes, but thought nothing of
it. Many Russians had never seen a Negro.

But a few minutes later, a man in plain clothes approached
me.

"Dokument!" he demanded.

"Document for what? I don't know you."

"Then come along with me to the station."

At the station, two blocks away, the plain-clothes man led
me into the office of the Nachalnik (Chief).

"Let me see your dokuments," he demanded.

I handed over my press card. He and the plain-clothes
man examined it closely and compared the picture in it
with my face. Apparently satisfied, the Nichalnik handed

it back and told me I could go. But I demanded an explanation.

"Vam nichevo Bespokoitsa (you have nothing to worry about)," the Nachalnik answered.

"But I think I have the right to know why I have been intercepted," I insisted.

The Nachalnik and the plain-clothes man looked at each other. "A citizen reported seeing you making drawings of the railway station and the bridge over the tracks at the trolleybus stop," the Nachalnik explained.

"Was the citizen a woman pushing a wheelbarrow?" I asked.

"Well, yes," he answered.

I opened my brief case and handed him my notebook, requesting him to find any drawings in it. I also proposed that he examine my brief case and search my person if he wished.

"I was merely jotting down the address and telephone number of a friend," I explained. "Here they are." I pointed to the address and telephone number in the notebook. "Furthermore, I would be a very inept spy to be making drawings of a railway station and bridge in broad daylight at a busy street corner."

"Forget about it," the Nachalnik said. Both he and the plain-clothes man extended their hands. I shook hands briefly.

However, during the next few days, as the alarming news began spreading that the Wehrmacht was soundly routing the Red Army, several of my foreign friends told me they had also been followed and intercepted on the streets. One British friend had even been pulled off a streetcar near the October Railway Station. Although I doubt that I could be suspected of being a German, it appeared that all foreigners were being looked upon as German spies.

Although I observed that the Russian rulers sought to express great surprise to the Russian people over the German attack, they could not truthfully claim that they had not been receiving timely warnings. Western intelligence sources had been reporting regularly to their own governments that Hitler was massing powerful forces in Poland near the Russian border and this information was being duly passed on to the Kremlin.

Shortly before the German attack, American Undersecretary of State Sumner Welles had passed on to Soviet Ambassador Konstantin Umansky substantiated information that Hitler was engaged in suspicious troop movements in the area of the Russian frontier. And, on April 19th, Sir Stafford Cripps, British Ambassador to Moscow, informed Soviet Foreign Minister Andrei Vyshinsky of German troop concentrations eastwards; as had British Foreign Secretary Anthony Eden alerted Soviet Ambassador Ivan Maisky in London.

Yet, despite all this, the Soviet government newspaper *Izvestia* had reported on June 14th: ". . . in the opinion of Soviet circles, rumors of Germany's intention to break the pact and begin an attack on the USSR are devoid of all foundation."

All these danger signals apparently were looked upon with contempt by the Kremlin, which appeared to be treating them as pestiferous capitalistic provocations. Insulated as they were from all foreign sources of information, the Russian people had no way of learning how threatening the situation actually was.

Only ten days before the German attack, the Russian people were told by Moscow Radio and the Soviet Press that "the press of foreign capitalistic countries is spreading rumors of an impending war between the Soviet Union and Germany. These absurd and untrue rumors are nothing but a clumsy propaganda maneuver of the forces arrayed against the Soviet Union and Germany which are interested in spreading and intensifying the war. . . ."

When Hitler's crushing blow struck ten days later, naturally the Russian people were astonished and stunned. They had been led to believe that the Soviet-German Non-Aggression Treaty of August 24, 1939, would protect them and now they were caught up in a psychoneurotic paroxyism that soon became contagious. The outward expression was near hysteria.

I blamed all this on the bungling, heedless and rigidly self-opinionated and vain Kremlin rulers. And I recalled the hide-bound Russian Communist who remarked proudly to me on the day the non-aggression pact was signed: "Our leaders have outsmarted those British and American capitalist intriguers."

Although the Germany Army was still a few hundred miles away from Moscow, war came dangerously close to me on the night of June 22nd. A high-explosive German air bomb fell in the courtyard of the building where I was living and the blast blew out all the windows of my fourth-floor apartment. Incendiary bombs rained down on the roof of the building and I joined the water bucket, sand and shovel brigade in extinguishing incipient fires. While my Russian male neighbors and I crawled about on the roof, powerful Russian searchlights knifed through the night sky seeking out Luftwaffe bombing planes. Ack-ack guns kept up a hellish chatter below in a field across the street.

Our building was in a highly vunerable location about midway between the nearby big Tushino military air base and Central Civil Airport. Down in the basement my wife and our women neighbors and their children huddled, some of them praying, despite the fact that for many years they had been subjected to constant and heavy anti-religious propaganda.

During the next few weeks I was to witness a continuing series of crushing defeats for the Red Army, despite the fact that the Russian rulers, at great sacrifice to the Russian people, had for two decades been preparing for war. Soviet Defense Commissar Klementi Voroshilov had often referred to the Red Army as being invincible. Indeed, the Russian people had so often been told of the invincibility of the Red Army that they had come to believe it.

But now, to their consternation, the really superb German Army Group Center was exploding that boast almost hourly, as it smashed its way toward Moscow. Stalin, seeking a soothing "explanation" for this debacle, in a radio broadcast on

July 3rd, made a right-about-face, declaring: "History shows that there are no invincible armies and never have been."

Disorganization and chaos reigned in the stunned and shattered Red Army. The Luftwaffe was smashing Russian planes by the hundreds caught grounded on airfields. German armor battered down Russian resistance as German planes strafed bewildered and reeling Red Army units from the air, creating terror and near-panic among Russian troops. Red Army supply services reached such a state of disorganization that ammunition, fuel for transport and shells for tanks and artillery often failed to arrive at the front.

So grave was the situation becoming that I was to see Stalin add terror from the rear to the terror being inflicted at the front by the Wehrmacht and Luftwaffe. In an effort to bolster up discipline and morale, he began looking for scapegoats for the Red Army's failures. Major-General A. A. Korobkov, Western Front Commander of the Russian 4th Army, and General A. G. Pavlov, Commander on the Western Front, and other high-ranking officers were ordered shot. With the same fate apparently awaiting them, several other high officers are known to have committed suicide. And those Russian soldiers who did risk escaping from German encirclement or captivity, ironically, were often rounded up by the MVD guards and accused of cowardice, desertion, or of being traitors.

About one month after the initial German attack, I was to see Stalin make an extraordinary ideological switch. Previously the Red Army had been referred to as the bulwark and shield of the ideals and aims of Communism; now the emphasis was suddenly shifted to the Patriotic War in defense of the Rodina (Native Land). The old pre-war rallying cries and slogans of vigilance, sacrifice and toil in the interest of Bolshevism, Communism, Marxism, Leninism and Stalinism were heard no more. Instead the Red Army soldiers were being exhorted to defend *sacred Russian soil* against the perfidious and brutal German invaders.

This quick changeover from defending a political concept to defending one's native soil did seem to have the desired effect. Discipline stiffened and there was a definite increase in the will to resist and sacrifice, both at the front and in the rear. Over the years I had come to learn how deeply Russians love their native soil, and I strongly believe that people are always more ready to undergo sacrifices in defending their native land than they are in defending any political ideology.

As summer passed into autumn, the German Army was rapidly approaching Moscow, even in the face of stubborn Russian resistance, and an aura of near-panic hung over everything. The first critical days came between October 10th and 19th. Stalin was determined that Moscow must not be captured by the Germans, and I heard Deputy Commissar of Foreign Affairs, S. A. Lozovsky, echo this at a press conference on October 11: "We shall not surrender Moscow."

But many Communist Party functionaries and policemen were quietly abandoning their offices and posts. A Russian friend of mine told me that the toilets at his factory had become inoperative and were found to be blocked with the torn Party cards of the factory's Communist Party members, since it was well known that captured Communists and Jews were summarily executed by Hitler's forces.

The remaining safe roads leading to the east were packed with masses of civilians lugging sacks and boxes and heading for the forests and steppeland to the east. Burglary and looting of vacated houses and apartments became widespread throughout the city. This was the period—in my opinion belated— when the foreign Diplomatic Corps was suddenly ordered to evacuate the city. The Press Department of the Foreign Ministry also ordered all foreign correspondents to leave Moscow at once.

There were increasingly grave doubts in some Kremlin circles that Moscow actually could be held. German armor had smashed through Russian defenses at Mozhaisk, about 60 miles west of Moscow, on the same road followed by Napoleon when he occupied Moscow in 1812. Additional barricades were thrown up in the city's streets as the Germans began massing forces, including a few thousand tanks, to storm the city.

All able-bodied Russian civilians were ordered to learn how to use guns and the Government newspaper *Izvestia*, on October 16th, appealed to the people to prepare to defend Moscow "from behind every stone . . . the enemy must be met with steel and fire." In short, bitter house-to-house street fighting if the Germans entered the city.

With their great talent for improvisation, the Russian authorities quickly assembled a special train for the dash eastward on October 16th. This train was to carry the Diplomatic Corps and the foreign correspondents through the wide gap that was still being held open to the east of Moscow. The destination was Kuibyshev, about 650 miles southeast on the Volga river.

Three days later I was still in Moscow, with the Germans battering at the beginning approaches to the city! My still being in besieged Moscow at this critical time meant, as a matter of unwritten record, that I remained in Moscow longer than any other foreign correspondent and at a time when the Germans had advanced closest on all fronts. German armor was expected to break into the city at any hour.

My presence in Moscow at this critical and agonizing time was not due to any bravery or journalistic stratagem on my part. Furthermore, I most certainly had no desire for the Nazi racists to get hold of me. Nevertheless, in retrospect, and for some reason which I then found and now find difficult to explain, I remained calm and devoid of any nervousness or fear. Perhaps I had acquired a large measure of the traditional fatalism of the Russian people.

The explanation for my still being there, when all my journalistic colleagues had evacuated the city, was simply that I and my wife had missed the special evacuation train. This happened through no fault of ours, and it did seem that we were trapped in the city, perhaps to fall into the hands of Hitler's Gestapo.

Of course, there was nothing to prevent our fleeing on foot, as tens of thousands of Russians were doing. But the icy Russian winter winds and snows had arrived early that year, as they had done when Napoleon captured Moscow in 1812, and the frigid steppe was not the most attractive of alternatives. The wolves were said to be exceedingly hungry that year; furthermore, Russian bears draw no color line.

At nine o'clock on the morning of October 16th, I had been notified by telephone to be at the Kazan Railway Station to board the special train at one P.M. Why had I missed it, when I had four hours to reach the station?

The answer is that Moscow's transportation system was by then wholly disrupted. All the other correspondents lived in the Metropole Hotel or near the center of the city, so reaching the railway station presented no problem to them. But I lived in the distant northern outskirts of Moscow. I had reckoned that the Metro (subway), which had a station near my house, could easily get my wife and me to the railway station in thirty minutes at the most.

We left the house for the subway station at exactly twelve o'clock. But to our great surprise, a militiaman stood guarding the locked doors of the Metro station, the subway had been closed! Streetcars and trolleybuses were running but irregularly, and besides, taking one of them was out of the question, for those that passed had people already hanging onto everything that could be grasped, including even one another.

What to do? We decided to begin walking, though there was scant likelihood of our ever reaching the railway station, which was on the other side of town, before the special train left. With all our baggage we could make only slow progress and by one o'clock, the scheduled departure time for our train, we were only one-third of the way to the railway station. I decided it would be useless to continue, so we turned toward the Metropole Hotel, the foreign correspondents' hangout.

The once teeming hotel was all but empty. Most of the chambermaids and waiters and porters had already left Moscow or been mobilized into civilian defense battalions. A new main floor desk clerk was on duty; the one I had known so well (he was a Jew) had also taken to the road eastward.

But the old bearded doorman, resplendent in his long blue and gold-trimmed overcoat, remained on duty at the door. He saluted me, opened the door and grabbed my wife's suitcase and ushered us into the lobby. Whereas normally it was next to impossible to find a vacant room in the Metropole, now there was a wide choice, from single rooms to luxurious suites.

Leaving my exhausted wife in the hotel, I went out for a stroll through the nearby streets. They were almost deserted. At the corner of Petrovka Street and Kuznetsky Most, I met an old Russian friend who worked in the city's largest electric power station. Though Petrov loved his country and her people, I had gained his confidence enough to know that he had a deep inner hatred of the Communist regime.

We walked together along Petrovka Street past the Bolshoi Theater and turned up Pushkin Street. At the corner of Khudozhestvenny Proyezd we met Boris Simonovich, another old friend. Boris was a lathe operator in the big Moscow ball bearing plant which Mussolini had built in exchange for Russian oil. That oil had been used in his war machine which invaded Ethiopia. We asked Boris to join us, and as we walked along we came to an Amerikanka, the name often used in Russia to designate a beer hall, so I invited my friends in for what might be our last drink together.

There were few customers in the place, which would normally have been crowded. We found a corner table, out of hearing distance of other customers, and gave the waiter our orders.

"My friend, I have known you for several years," Petrov said to me as we settled over our glasses of vodka and black bread and bologna. "You know my country and my people well, for you have lived among us as a brother. You have seen us go through the starvation years of the mid-thirties. You are well acquainted with the privations and hardships my people have endured.

"Over the years the Communist regime let the people face hunger, inadequately clothed and housed, so most of our national income could be devoted to building heavy industry. Our Bolshevik rulers said this was necessary in order to build our country's defensive might against capitalist encirclement and prepare for the inevitable struggle between socialism and capitalism. We were continually told that the Red Army was being kept in a state of full military preparedness and that it was invincible. We were assured that any attacker would be repulsed and destroyed on his own territory. Now see what is happening."

I looked over at Boris.

"All that Petrov says is quite true," Boris stated. "Although the official communiques don't say so, we know that our supposedly invincible Red Army, built from the sweat, blood and privation of our people, is being soundly beaten and driven back by the Germans. Our people in the battle zones might have been of some help, but the Communist government never permitted them to own guns.

"You know as well as I do that the Germans are now closing in on the gates of Moscow. I wouldn't be surprised if our Kremlin people won't soon be begging capitalist Britain and America for help."

As a matter of fact, although unknown to the Russian people, Stalin actually had already suggested to Churchill that 25 or 30 British divisions would be welcome in Russia. He had also informed President Roosevelt's personal envoy, Harry Hopkins, that American troops would also be welcome. We

know now that as far back as July, Stalin already was demanding a second front in the West.

By now the beer hall was empty, except for us, and the bar-
man came over with folded arms.

"When are you going to close shop, Popov?" Petrov asked.

"I have no intention of closing," Popov answered. "I know
the Germans love beer and I intend doing a big business after
they arrive."

Popov wanted to know what I thought of the situation. I
admitted that the situation was critical but all was not yet lost,
for Russia now had powerful allies in the West. Even if Moscow fell to the Germans, it need not necessarily mean the end
of the war, nor the capitulation of Russia.

My two friends and I parted at the door of the Amerikanka
and I returned to the Metropole Hotel. Reports were circulating everywhere that the Germans were still advancing and
Russian defenses melting away like icicles under a warm
spring sun.

In the lobby I overheard the following repartee between two
Russians, obviously in a fatalistically light mood:

"Tovarisch Kuznetsov, what in the world can the Red Army
be doing out there?" asked the first.

"Devil take it, it's out there no doubt," answered the other,
"But a refugee that I saw this morning told me it's advancing
backwards on Moscow."

There was something unusual and unprecedented about the
way Russians were talking out loud about the situation. Most
Russians had serious doubts that Moscow could be held, and
it had leaked out that some important people in the Kremlin
felt the same way. This, it appeared to me, had removed most
of the fear of the dread MVD, and loosened the tongues of
ordinary Russians.

There was no doubt that the Red Army was resisting as best
it could, in spite of the tremendous losses inflicted on it by the
Germans. Casualties—dead, wounded or captured—were re-

ported to have already reached more than two million, a figure far greater than had been suffered by any army over the same period of time in the history of warfare.

Russian superiority over the Germans in tanks and planes had largely been decimated. During the first months of the war, Russia lost more than two thousand planes and the thousands of tanks that Stalin had deployed along the front west of Moscow were reported to have been cut down to less than five hundred.

The privations, hardships and losses which Red Army troops were experiencing would probably have proved demoralizing to western soldiers. But they were more or less routine for Russian troops. The overwhelming majority were of hardy peasant stock who all their lives had toiled from dawn to dusk, and often after dusk, on the soil of the limitless Russian steppes. Additionally, since 1917 the Russian people had experienced a woeful lack of the creature comforts and necessities of life. But it took more than physical stamina to match Hitler's powerful motorized and mechanized war machine.

CHAPTER XV

Deadheading to the Volga

O, thou Volga, Mother stream, O, thou river broad and deep.
—From Volga Boat Song

A S A MATTER OF FORMALITY, on October 17th, I decided to report to the Press Department of the Ministry of Foreign Affairs, though I had slight hope of finding any officials there.

"They all left yesterday on the special train for Kuibyshev," the old elevator operator told me. "But there is one official up in the Protocol Department."

I handed this official my press card for identification purposes. He quickly reacted by demanding, "What are you doing here? Why didn't you leave yesterday on the special train?"

I explained my predicament, apparently to his satisfaction.

"I'll have to get you out of town somehow, but I don't know how," he remarked, turning to the telephone. He called someone at the railroad station and after talking for a few minutes hung up.

"Go down there and see the stationmaster. I'll try to get you a car."

He then telephoned to the Government Garage.

"I've got to have a car immediately!" he shouted into the telephone.

I could hear someone shouting as loudly at the other end.

"But you must find one. There is an inostrany korrespondent (foreign correspondent) here that I must send to the railway station. Hurry!"

Knowing the Russian language well—and when Russians are excited they speak loudly over the telephone—I had followed most of the dialogue. Exasperated, the official handed me the telephone. "Gospodin (Mister) Smith, you talk with him."

Hearing my unmistakable foreign accent, the garageman seemed convinced. The car arrived in the autum murk within twenty minutes and I instructed the chauffeur to drive me to the Kazan Railway Station.

I found the entire main waiting room floor covered with a mass of Red Army soldiers resting or sleeping on their knapsacks. They seemed calm, resigned and dog-tired. Civilians found difficulty in not stepping on them as they crossed the blacked-out station.

The platforms in the train sheds were congested with a mass of civilians amid suitcases, boxes, sacks and bundles. Off in the distance, reddish glares from fires set by German incendiary bombs could be seen. Searchlights pierced the sky, often catching in their powerful beams barrage balloons floating like silvery, distorted bologna sausages over the besieged city.

Although at the time I did not seem to be conscious of the great danger, I later realized that this railway station—the last operative station in the city—which Stalin was determined to keep in operation, was the only rail terminus from the east and presented an important strategic target for the Luftwaffe. Through this station Stalin was pouring troops, many of them from distant Siberia and bound for the front. Had a German bomb been dropped on the station, the slaughter would have been ghastly. Plus the thousands of soldiers, civilians thronged to it because it was the last rail escape from Moscow.

With great difficulty I found my way to the stationmaster's office on the second floor. It was besieged by frantic people but I managed to wedge my way inside. When I presented my press card to the weary railway official, he said that the Foreign Ministry had telephoned about me.

Manifestly, there were no train schedules, but he offered me a place in a freight car carrying important documents. But this train's destination was top secret and even the stationmaster said he did not know its destination. Naturally, I refused. Nobody could tell me where this freight train was going. Most likely it was going deep into the interior of the country, perhaps over the Ural Mountains into Siberia, and that was the last place I wanted to be.

"Tomorow night I expect to dispatch a train of passenger cars—if the Red Army can hold the line open," the stationmaster went on. "Be at the station not later than ten o'clock."

I had asked the chauffeur to wait for me, but he evidently had business elsewhere, for when I came out of the station he was gone. Through darkened streets I found my way back to the Metropole. Just as I arrived, the air raid sirens whined and, together with my wife, I dashed into the hotel's basement.

The next day was October 18th. Upon going into the street that morning, I found the panic growing in intensity. Everybody was talking about the Luftwaffe raid of the previous night. Stragglers from the front zone were reporting that the Red Army was still being pounded back and on the Volokolamsk Highway, northwest of the city, advance German units were reported to be only twenty miles from the city limits.

I observed two distinct types of people in Moscow at that time—those who were still evacuating toward the eastern outskirts and those who had decided to remain. The former had drawn faces and were always lugging baggage; the latter appeared relatively carefree, as if waiting to welcome the Ger-

mans. I heard one of them remark in the Metropole Hotel
lobby, "Eat, drink and be merry, for tomorrow, or day after
tomorrow, the Germans will be here. But they can't possibly be
any worse than the Bolsheviks."

One of these carefree non-evacuees offered to deliver to
my room gold watches, diamond rings, Persian carpets and
gold plate—but only for American dollars. The ruble, it appeared, no longer held any attraction. I felt convinced that he
had been engaged in the widespread looting of recent days, in-
tending to unload the spoils to the Germans after they occupied
Moscow.

As dusk was falling, the Foreign Ministry official telephoned
and instructed me to be at the Ministry at nine o'clock with
my wife and baggage. A car would take us to the railway station. On this my last day in besieged Moscow, the city was full
of the tenseness, of the feel and smell of war. My journalistic
colleagues had departed three days before and were now hi-
bernating in Kuibyshev. I wondered if they were curious about
what had happened to me.

Upon arriving at the railway station, I found the scene much
the same as it had been the day before; only the individual
soldiers and civilians had changed. I found my way again to the
stationmaster's office. He immediately recognized me and assured me that we could leave on a train scheduled to depart for
Kuibyshev at midnight. Neither money nor ticket would be
necessary.

I and my wife lugged our baggage to the indicated platform.
An airraid alarm was on, but nobody seemed to pay much
attention. Nowhere did I see any signs indicating the way to
shelters. We sat on our baggage alongside the coach we had
been instructed to board. As on my previous visit, there was
the very real possibility of mass slaughter if a German air
bomb should fall on the station.

The alert continued until well after midnight. The stampede
to board the coach, when the signal was given, was worse than

the rush hour on the New York subway. The coach, with all the shades sealed down for blackout purposes, was quickly filled with a motley array of Russians of all ages, sexes and callings. A place meant anywhere one could wedge into, either in the compartments or in the corridor. Might meant right, and my wife and I stood aside. We had no desire to get our ribs broken.

When the grand rush had ended, we clambered aboard. The coach was a "hard wagon"—that is, naked board seats facing each other in each compartment. No seat cushions. On Russian railways "hard wagon" means literally hard.

The only standing room was in front of the smelly toilet at the end of the corridor. We resigned ourselves to the circumstances. Yet we certainly did not relish the thought of having to travel, for how many days we did not know, standing before this stinking water closet. Fortunately, the weather was already cold and this promised to lessen the stench somewhat.

The train crept along slowly through the yards at what seemed like ten miles an hour—a sitting duck for a Luftwaffe bomber. The usually loud-talking Russians conversed in muted tones. A few hours later, I was agreeably surprised to find a Russian friend and his wife occupying places on one of the hard seats.

With the usual kindness and deference to foreigners, especially if the foreigners happened also to be friends, the husband made a proposal. He and his wife would stand in the corridor each alternate four hours and allow us to sit in their seats for four hours. This was a welcome and much appreciated arrangement.

As much as twelve hours were spent at some stations waiting for the right-of-way, for military trains had priority. By the fourth day our food supplies had been exhausted, and we were still closer to Moscow than to Kuibyshev. But luckily there were many peasants at all way-stations offering to sell us boiled chickens, roasted meat, milk and honey, boiled eggs, fruit, baked bread and other foodstuffs.

My wife and I had prepared for every eventuality. We had packed our suitcases with certain articles that we knew would be in short supply in the countryside—sugar, tea and coffee, soap, nylon stockings and woolen socks, shirts and underwear, towels and handkerchiefs. We felt that such commodities might outrank rubles in purchasing power, and we were soon to learn that they did.

The few thousand rubles that I had in my pocket held no attraction for the peasants and they categorically refused to accept them. Everywhere I offered my rubles, the answer was always the same: *"Nyet, Gospodin, rubles nyet!"*

What had happened to the money that the Soviet Government had often called "the world's soundest currency"? Russian peasants, it was obvious, were convinced that the Germans would win the war and they felt that the ruble would soon become worthless. They suspected that their next currency would be German marks.

It was then that the contents of our baggage came to the rescue. We began bartering tea and sugar, coffee and soap, nylon stockings and woolen socks, shirts and underwear for foodstuffs. Soap had a very high barter value and luckily we had a large supply; sugar, tea and coffee also traded well. And my wife's nylon stockings had great appeal for the young female peasants.

But to my great surprise, the few bottles of vodka we had seemed to hold little appeal. My wife told me the reason; Russian peasants were expert brewers of *samogon,* a home distilled form of bootleg vodka.

At several stations I saw long trains of flatcars loaded with valuable lathes and other industrial machinery. They had no protective covering from the autumn rains and snow. This equipment, which was being evacuated from factories in the Ukraine to the Urals and Siberia, was rusting from exposure.

The metal plates on most of it showed that it had been made in the United States, Germany or England.

Many of the stations that we reached were virtual cesspools. The hundreds of trains going in both directions, in addition to those that had spent long hours in the yards, had emptied their water closets between the rails. The minute you stepped off the coach you sank to the shoetops in this mire. It was thanks only to the weather being so cold that the stench was not highly offensive and that disease of epidemic proportions was prevented from breaking out.

During a layover at a station near Penza, my attention was attracted by three steel-gray cars coupled to a train standing on a parallel track, headed in the opposite direction. Near the ends on each side of the cars I noticed steel-barred windows, about two feet square, high under the roofs. Peering out were emaciated human faces, some of them pleading in a strange language that I did not understand. They were obviously in distress.

My first thought was that they might be German and Romanian prisoners of war. But through discreet inquiry in the railway yards, I learned that they were actually civilian prisoners who had been arrested en masse by the Soviet Secret Police in Bessarabia, Northern Bucovina and in the Ukraine. The charges were "enemies of the people," "counter revolutionaries" or suspicion of being "anti-Soviet and Pro-German." (Bessarabia and Northern Bucovina were formerly Romanian, forcibly annexed by Russia in 1940, and the Ukraine has always had a strong nationalist movement seeking independence from Great Russia.)

Day after day the train crawled slowly over the flat Russian steppeland, stopping for hours on sidetracks at every sizable town. On the eleventh day after leaving besieged Moscow, I arrived in Kuibyshev. My baggage was almost empty, but I had a full stomach, though I was sorely in need of a bath.

When I made a sudden appearance among the other correspondents, Henry Shapiro, veteran United Press correspondent in Moscow, remarked, "So, you lucky fellow, the Russians have been favoring you. They let you stay in Moscow. We wanted to stay, too, but they made us leave."

I explained my predicament, assuring them that I would have gladly exchanged places with them, but they remained unconvinced.

During my first week in Kuibyshev, I came across an old American Negro woman named Williana Burroughs who was a veteran member of the American Communist Party. She had been evacuated earlier from Moscow and was continuing in Kuibyshev, her work as announcer for the broadcasts of Radio Moscow beamed to the United States.

She and a British woman announcer had been provided with a small room in a cold basement on Kuibyshev Street. The old Negro woman was obviously undernourished and inadequately clothed—as, of course, were tens of thousands of other evacuees in Kuibyshev—to face the bitter cold that had begun sweeping down from Siberia and across the Volga River onto the city.

Feeling sorry for the old woman, I often bought a few bottles of vodka in the special Diplomatic Shop, which was open to foreign correspondents, and turned them over to her. This "Moscow mule" she did not drink, but used more profitably to trade for food, and perhaps warm second-hand clothes, at the public market or among private individuals.

Back in Moscow, after the war, the old woman confided to me that she had had enough of life in Russia. She left soon thereafter for America and shortly after her arrival in New York she died. The neglect and hardships she had experienced during the war undoubtedly hastened her death. But I did feel personally that what help I had been able to give her during those harsh war days did contribute somewhat toward enabling her to survive to return to die in her native land.

Meanwhile, I was learning from a distance that the fierce

battle for Moscow continued to rage with unabated fury. Two giants were locked in desperate and bloody combat, like two dinosaurs of the Mesozoic era.

The Germans were so convinced that they would soon capture Moscow that Hitler, I learned, had invited Mussolini to join him in a victory parade on Red Square, culminating in a grand banquet in the Kremlin.

But the Russians were equally determined not to surrender Moscow. To the Russians Moscow had now become not the citadel of world Communism, but Mother Moscow, cradle of ancient Muscovy.

A few weeks more and the issue would be decided one way or another, with the odds now apparently slowly turning against the Germans. Hitler's great 4th Army, which had borne the brunt of the spearheading toward Moscow, had now spent itself against the increasing and almost superhuman resistance of the Red Army, and at a time when German officers could see the city's onion-shaped church domes and Kremlin towers through powerful field glasses. And Russia's perennial ally—winter—was now about to harass and torment the Germans.

CHAPTER XVI

Down on the Farm:
Collective Style

Bowed by the weight of centuries he leans
Upon his hoe and gazes on the ground
—Edwin Markham, *The Man With The Hoe*

WITH MUCH UNPRODUCTIVE TIME on my hands in the late summer of 1942, life in Kuibyshev was becoming boresome and tedious. I was tired of bumping into the same old friends, of watching the mighty Volga, Russia's "Mississippi" "jes rollin' along," of reading the same Soviet war communiqués day in and day out. I began thinking of some way of gaining respite from it all, if only for a few days.

Kuibyshev was located in one of Russia's richest agricultural regions, so I was sure that there must be collective farms nearby. What about using this lull to "bury" myself down on the farm? I could relax from the anxieties of war and the humdrum life in a Russian provincial town. Besides I might come up with a good story.

But like everything else in Russia, one does not just pack one's baggage, buy a ticket and go where one wishes. Everything has to be arranged through proper official channels. I had access to those channels and made my wishes known—first obtaining assurances that no trips to the front were in the offing. My request was approved, but there remained the problem of transportation. I would have to wait.

One hot summer day I was notified that a farm truck would be in the city the next day and that arrangements could be made for me to hitch a ride. That suited me, so early the following afternoon I was jogging along over a rutted road across the steppe for the twenty-five mile ride to the Kuibyshev Collective Farm.

The truck driver was a woman about thirty years old named Zoya. Zoya was busty, husky and looked rusty—perhaps from constant exposure to the hot steppe sun. She had her straw-colored hair covered with a large silk handkerchief, handled her truck like an old hand and was loquacious. Since I spoke Russian, it was not a one way conversation.

"Could I help with the driving?" I asked.

"No, thank you," Zoya answered. "I've been doing this for a long time and I am not tired. Besides, I am held strictly responsible for this machine. If you should break it, they wouldn't do anything to you. They would punish me for allowing Socialist property to be damaged."

When I saw a large oak tree looming in the distance, I suggested that Zoya stop there for refreshments. I had some sandwiches and two bottles of vodka in my bag. I also had a thermos of piping hot coffee that my wife had prepared. We parked under the tree and ate our sandwiches. And like any Russian, male or female, Zoya was not averse to taking a few drafts of vodka to help wash down the sandwiches. As for the coffee, Zoya said she had not had any real coffee for years.

"We make better vodka, though, on the farm," Zoya remarked, as she downed her third. To stop Russian muzhiks (peasants) from drinking their beloved vodka would be just as difficult as trying to prevent Frenchmen and Italians from drinking wine.

We wheezed into the main street of the farm village two hours after leaving Kuibyshev. Zoya delivered me to the house of the president (manager) of the collective. This functionary was not at home, but his wife had been informed of my expected arrival. She welcomed me into the three-room house with traditional Russian hospitality and soon had zakuska (snacks) on the table.

"Make yourself at home," she said. "Boris Borisovitch had to go out into the field but he will be back before dark."

At dusk the husband rolled up in a dusty and rattly old Russian "Ford" car.

"Ah, drug (friend; pronounced droog), you must pardon me for not being at home to welcome you," he apologized, as he entered the house. "I got word that one of the tractors had broken down and had to go to see that it was repaired as quickly as possible. You know, this war is making us short of both tractors and parts. We must do much improvising. If we find that one tractor is hopeless, we cannibalize it to keep the others going."

Boris Borisovitch suggested that we relax for the evening and tomorrow he would take me for an excursion over a part of the farm. After a heavy meal of borsch (Russian soup made of beetroot, cabbage and meat), corn on the cob, pelmeni (meat dumplings), black bread and numerous cups of tea (Russians are among the world's biggest tea drinkers), we moved to chairs out in the front yard. Though I had been city raised, I pretended to understand everything about farming.

Looking out toward the field, I saw flickering lights at a great distance.

"I see you have a few fireflies here," I remarked.

"No, Tovarisch, those are not fireflies," Boris Borisovitch laughed. "We work here day and night. What you are seeing are lights from our tractors and other farm machines.

I was given a verbal preview of the farm. It was a millionaire collective farm, I was told, meaning that it had an annual agricultural income valued at more than one million rubles. It was one of the largest in the middle Volga region, sprawling over an area almost as large as Cook County, Illinois. One thousand persons, including men, women and children normally belonged to the farm. But they were now short-handed due to the war.

There were no fixed wages, the farmers being compensated on the basis of the number of work-days actually performed. Everything on the farm was owned in common, except the Motor-Tractor Stations (MTS), which was owned by the state and its services had to be paid for in kind. A fixed quota of the farm's output had to be delivered to the Soviet Government; anything over and above this could be disposed of or divided up among the members of the collective. They did not own the land; it had been merely put at their disposal "in perpetuity" by the Soviet Government. (I have used state and government interchangeably; the state, Soviet Government and the Communist Party are one large interlocking directorate, with the Communist Party doing all the directing.)

The collective was so large that the farmers often spent several days away from the village. They lived in box-car-like barracks on wheels alongside the fields and prepared and ate their meals on long rough board tables outside.

My host aroused me at daybreak the next morning, saying we would have to leave early if we hoped to return by nightfall. After a hearty breakfast of porridge, eggs turned over, blini (pancakes)—Boris Borisovitch suggested a stout draft of vodka "for the road."

The fields came right down to the village, with the common household crops—cabbage, tomatoes, onions, turnips, beets, radishes, corn, etc.—planted on the outskirts. Also, each household had been allotted its own small garden plot.

After traveling for several miles through fields of wheat undulating like golden waves in the breeze, and looking not unlike the vast wheat fields on the Great Plains states back home, we came to a MTS. These stations were introduced by Stalin as complementing his farm collectivization program.

All the farm machinery—tractors, harvesters, reapers and trucks—were controlled, serviced and operated by the MTS. In return, the farm paid a stipulated fee in produce for this service. This gave the MTS great authority and power on the collective farm, inasmuch as the prosperity and fulfillment of any production plan depended greatly on the cooperation of the MTS. Khrushchev, incidently, disbanded the MTS in 1958 and sold all its machinery to the collectives.

The machines—or what was left of them—appeared to be in very bad condition, but still serviceable. Those out in the field were wheezing along and doing their jobs, but just barely. The machines at the station were being repaired and serviced, evidently by temporary mechanics, who obviously were working by rule of trial and error. All the best mechanics had long since been mobilized into the Red Army.

In a discussion with one of the mechanics, I found that he had little knowledge of agriculture in any other country. For example, he was firmly convinced that Russian farming used far more tractors than American. I told him that American farmers owned about six million tractors, as compared with the one million five hundred thousand in use on Russian farms. His reaction amounted to "don't try to kid me." I made no effort to pursue the matter further; after all, I was the guest of a war-time ally who was bearing the brunt of the struggle against Hitler Germany.

Despite the richness of its soil and the admittedly large amount of mechanical farm machinery, Russia's agricultural output per capita lagged behind America's and still does. Indeed, Russia is now buying wheat from America and anywhere else it can be found. For the years 1955–58, per capita grain production in Russia was 1,256 pounds; in the United States it was 1,958 pounds. For the same period, the United States was producing 245 pounds of vegetables per capita, as compared with Russia's 122. In Russia meat production averaged

74 pounds, while the United States was producing 203 pounds.

Russia's agricultural operations struck me as being inefficient and bureaucratic. Facts are stubborn things, and they now reveal that farming in the Soviet Union today continues to be just as inefficient. As an example, one American farmer produces enough to feed 27 persons, while a Russian farmer can produce only enough to feed five. And it takes 22 per cent of Russia's population to raise enough food for its population, compared with about four per cent for the United States.

This inefficiency appears to persist, despite the fact that there has been an enormous increase in the amount of available farming machinery since I was last there.

By three o'clock in the afternoon, we had arrived at a distant farm brigade's headquarters, just as it was gathering for lunch. Only women and old men and young boys and girls were present; all the young able-bodied men were away at war —and many of the younger women, too.

I joined in the lunch, which consisted of potato soup, with some bits of meat in it, black bread, pelmini, milk and jam— not a very rich fare, yet nobody seemed undernourished or hungry. Russian peasants are a hardy lot.

I was shown the inside of the barrack-like sleeping quarters. There were two tiers of bunks on each side, with the female sleeping area in one half and the male in the other.

Several other work brigades were visited later in the day— and each had much the same sleeping and living arrangements. My host asked each brigade leader how the work was coming along, if anything was needed, if the quota was being fulfilled, if there were any complaints. No complaints were made in my presence.

I had been introduced as an American newspaper correspondent. With no radios and not having been back to the village for several days, many of the farm workers wanted to know how the war was going. Others asked when the Western Allies were going to open a second front in Europe.

"There will be a second front," I assured them. "I am certain that preliminary plans are now being drawn up for an invasion of Europe."

"But when?" an old muzhik asked anxiously. "After Russia has been bled white?"

It was now time to start back, my host suggested, and his timing was accurate, for we rolled into the village just at dusk —covered with a thin layer of brown dust.

"Come, quick, get that dirt off," my hostess demanded, as she led me to an enameled wash-basin beside which stood a large pitcher of water and a bar of laundry soap.

Meanwhile, she was setting on the table a meal of borsch, potatoes, fried chicken, and a samovar of boiling water for making tea.

During our meal I asked my host something about himself.

"I am a gorodskoi chelovek (city man). I am an exfactory worker from Kuibyshev."

I could not restrain from asking very tactfully how it happened that a city-born factory worker was now managing a huge farm.

"Well, it's like this, Tovarisch Smith," he responded. "You see, I am an old Communist Party member and we Communists are more developed politically, more capable of leadership. That's why the Party sent me here to manage this collective. The Party has the fullest confidence in me."

I did not pursue that matter further, but it did seem odd to me that the Party did not have enough confidence in any real dirt farmers to entrust them with the management of this giant Kolkhoz (collective farm). Yet, the regime was being consistent. The proletarian factory workers had to keep an eye on the individualistic peasants, for Lenin had once warned that "either we choke the peasants or they choke us."

The next day I was shown over the village, which had only

one long dusty main street with almost identical planed log houses on one side and huge barns on the other. At the head of the street stood an ancient church, its gilded, onion-shaped dome glistening in the sun. It was now being used as a storehouse for grain, potatoes and fodder. There were no bells in the belfry—they had been melted down for bullets during the Revolution.

The only comparatively new buildings were the combination kindergarten-nursery-school and the farm club. The children seemed rosy-faced and healthy. The headmistress was a Moscow schoolteacher who had evacuated herself from Moscow at the height of the Nazi push. She told me there were two hundred children under her care and that they saw their mothers on the average only about once a week.

The farmers' houses, all painted rusty brown, in the old pre-Revolution style, were so alike that seeing one was like seeing them all. There were plain cloth curtains at the windows, a rough wooden table covered with an oil cloth in the front room and a silk shade over the naked electric light bulb hanging above it. Two very disparate objects were found in almost all the houses—an icon in a corner of the front room and a picture of Stalin hanging on a wall as far away from the icon as possible.

Each house, of course, contained the inevitable combination Russian stove—made of whitewashed bricks and serving for both cooking and heating in winter. During severe winter weather, Russians in the rural areas sleep on top of these stoves.

Back of each house was a lean-to in which the farmer kept his own cow, chickens, goats, geese, ducks and hogs. About forty feet beyond these stood unpainted box-like "sentries"—hole-in-the-ground privies. Down a slope beyond the privies was the village pond, where ducks and geese glided over its glassy surface—the scene was like a page out of Gogol or Turgenev.

By the third day I had seen about all there was to be seen. I had planned on spending about three days idling away the time under a tree on the bank of the pond, letting the war and the rest of the world go by, but my host informed me that he was going to Kuibyshev the next day. There would not be another truck going to the city for about a week, so I decided to go back with him.

Within two hours I was back in Kuibyshev perusing the war communiqués that my wife had been collecting and saving for me—and trying to explain to my inquisitive colleagues where I had been these past few days.

This divertisement at the grassroots once again convinced me of the innate humaneness, hospitality and unsophistication of the ordinary Russian people, something that even long years of exposure to Communist anti-foreign propaganda has not been able to eradicate.

Long and intimate contact with the Russian common man has convinced me that they bear no enmity towards the American people, nor do I believe, really, that many Americans harbor any antagonism against them.

CHAPTER XVII

Kuibyshev Interval

Pull away, boys, pull away, home we'll reach before the night.
—Volga Boat Song

BEFORE THE WAR, Kuibyshev had been little heard of outside Russia. If the city had been known at all in Europe and America, it was by its centuries-old name of Samara—the city had been renamed Kuibyshev after one of Lenin's most trusted Commissars during the civil war that followed the Revolution. Now since the Soviet Government, the foreign diplomatic corps, the foreign correspondents and other foreigners had been rushed from besieged Moscow to this old Volga River city, Kuibyshev was becoming a world-wide date line.

Kuibyshev—old Samara—was a typical Russian provincial city—unkempt, dusty and dull. But its location on a slope overlooking the Volga had its geographical attractions; one could look out across this storied Russian river toward what seemed an endless steppe on the eastern side and conjure up visions of Genghis Khan and his marauding Tartar hordes dashing to the Volga on their stout Tartar ponies.

Normally the city had a population of about three hundred thousand. Evacuees had now swollen the population to almost one million and this rapid population increase had created frightful congestion. The problem of feeding this influx was serious. And there was only one third-class hotel, the Grand, on the main thoroughfare, Kuibyshev Street. Some of the minor diplomats and the foreign correspondents were packed into this dingy pre-Revolution building. But through friendly contacts, my wife and I managed to find quarters elsewhere in the city.

Holes in the sidewalks made walking dangerous during the blackout. Here and there were a few new, pretentiously ugly Soviet-built structures. But the overwhelming majority were solid and tasteful buildings of the Czarist vintage. After all, Samara had once been the capital of the province of the same name; it had been a garrison town, a river shipping port, its levee packed with grain, cattle and dairy products. It had been a great roistering center for the lustful, vodka-guzzling Cossacks of the area.

One of the most unusual things about Kuibyshev was that, though it was an old Russian city, it showed evidence of planning—something quite rare in old Russian cities. It was founded in 1586, yet its right-angled streets were as straight as a ruler. Kuibyshev lay on one of the old trade routes to the Khiva and Bokhara and farther into the East. In the seventeenth century Kalmyk Tartars had besieged the city; now, in the twentieth, it was being "invaded" by another motley array of foreigners.

The city contained many contrasts. Rows of log houses, with ginger-bread door and window frames, looking alike as two ducks, lined most of the streets, flush with the sidewalks. Yet one could also find French classic, Italian Renaissance, Empire, Byzantine and Scandinavian styles of architecture here and there in the city. The large Catholic Church was genuine Gothic. And then there were the comparatively new Soviet buildings—box-like and painted steel gray. There was also the huge opera house on a large square, with its Corinthian-topped columns.

I began making contacts, both foreign and Russian, as every correspondent must do if he wants to be kept well informed on what is happening. My first diplomatic call was at the Australian Legation, which occupied the second floor of a building on Kuibyshev Street. And it was from a window of this Legation that I was to see a depressing sight—depressing both for me and for members of the Legation.

While sitting one day with the Australian Minister, the Press Attaché and another member of the staff, we heard the tread of marching feet in the street below. Going to a window, we looked down with amazement on hundreds of men and women, boys and girls, being marched under guard by uniformed men armed with rifles and pistols.

"Holy smokes!" exclaimed one of the Australians, "I hadn't expected to see anything like that!"

What we were witnessing were prisoners—citizens arrested on suspicion of disloyalty or for some criticism of the bad living or food conditions, which made them suspect of being pro-German.

Incidentally, the Australian Legation was the only diplomatic mission in Russia with a labor attaché on its staff. This attaché told me that he had been sent by his government in the hope that he could establish a close wartime liaison with Soviet trade union officials. But after trying; unsuccessfully for many months, he left the country with his mission unfulfilled.

A few days later, while sitting by a window in the Grand Hotel with a western diplomat, another convoy of similar prisoners passed. My host remarked that this was not the first time he had seen such a melancholy sight.

"But why do they have to march them through the main street?" he asked. "Well, I suppose it's done to throw fear into the hearts of any other Russians who might have similar leanings. But it certainly does create a highly unfavorable impression on the foreign colony."

The next day, when I went to the Press Department of the

Foreign Ministry to submit a cable for censorship, I asked one
of the censors with whom I was on quite friendly terms why it
was necessary. He agreed that it was "unwise" and "politically
injudicious." And he must have passed this observation on
through proper channels, for neither I nor any other foreigners
afterward ever saw convoys of civilian prisoners being marched
through Kuibyshev Street again.

One of the continual irritations of foreigners living in the
Grand Hotel was the plumbing. Often there was no water, hot
or cold. The bathroom hot water tanks refused to function
regularly, and a "booking list" had to be arranged for guests
wanting to bathe.

Many of the foreigners, accustomed to bathing regularly,
discovered a large public bathhouse a few blocks away. Crowds
of Russians, many of them officers and soldiers, flocked there
from dawn to late at night. But a militiaman at the entrance,
upon spotting a foreigner, usually managed to clear a path
through the crowd for him. There was no running hot water
in the building where my wife and I lived, so we took our regular baths there, too. My being a foreigner—and a colored one
at that—made this quick and easy.

This public bathhouse, I found, was not classless in a supposedly classless society. It had, to my knowledge, three cate-
gories—first, second and third. This meant that low-paid Russian civilians and soldiers could gain access only to the large
general bath-hall. Better-paid functionaries and army officers
could enjoy the privacy or semiprivacy of the first and second
class baths, with towels and soap supplied and with attendants
available to scrub their backs and rub them down.

One of the more attractive "fixtures" at the Grand Hotel was
a busty, curvaceous and flaxen-haired desk clerk. She was in
her early thirties, spoke three non-Russian languages and was a
good mixer. I recalled having seen her before in hotels in Moscow frequented by foreigners, but she was not a desk clerk then.

The attention of an important attache in the British Em-

bassy focused on this comely blond. It soon became obvious
that he liked her and she reciprocated. I used often to see them,
between acts, promenading happily together around the foyer
of the Kuibyshev Opera House. This Britisher seemed to pride
himself over having outsmarted his foreign colleagues in "capturing" this good-looking blond.

To me, already an old Russia hand and wise to the wiles
often employed for certain ends, my presumption was that it
was this lady who had done the "capturing." I had learned long
ago from well-informed Russian sources that this innocent
looking lady had done espionage work in Spain during the
Spanish Civil War and was still doubtlessly engaged in her
trade. The British attaché was a friend of mine, and not wanting to disrupt his blissful days on the Volga, I never mentioned
this to him.

My wife had managed to find a seamstress who lived on the
first floor of an apartment house in the northern section of
Kuibyshev. One day I accompanied her to the seamstress'
apartment, through a window of which I noticed a high board
fence topped with barbed wire. I casually asked what was behind it.

"Prisoners," she answered dryly, without going into any
further detail. I did not press her for any added information,
but the next day I went early in the morning to a peasant market next door to the high fence. As I arrived, long lines of boys,
none more than eighteen years old, were being marched out of
the lot under armed guard. I followed at a respectable distance;
the boys were loaded onto a barge on the Volga. I presumed
they had been forcibly mobilized and were being shipped away
to do forced labor in a rear zone.

Then there was also the case of the young Spaniards, which
I had learned about through well-informed Russian friends.
These young Spaniards, who had been given refuge in Moscow
after the Spanish Civil War, had also been mobilized into a war
plant on the outskirts of Kuibyshev. The boys, who had been

about fifteen years old when they arrived in Moscow, found their working and living conditions almost unbearable. The food situation even worse. And unlike the Russians, who had become conditioned to accepting such hardships and keeping quiet, the young Spaniards were outspoken in expressing their discontent.

They were arrested at once and jailed by the Secret Police. But they did not remain in jail long, because of the presence in Kuibyshev of a powerful Spanish Communist—Dolores Ibarruri, La Passionara. She herself was a refugee from the wrath of Franco and was in high favor with Stalin. Through her intercession, the young Spaniards were soon released. Had she not interceded, the outcome might have been quite different.

A diplomatic stir in foreign circles and commotion in Russian official circles occurred when the American Ambassador, Admiral William Standley, reminded Russian authorities that it did not seem that the Russian people were being fully informed of the enormous and vital supply of military and other aid arriving from the United States for the Russian war effort against the Germans.

The Russian authorities reacted by making known publicly though half-heartedly that aid was being received from America, but they did make known adequately and fully the great extent of this indispensable American assistance.

Another great stir was caused in western diplomatic circles in Kuibyshev when the Soviet Government informed the Polish Embassy that its presence was not welcome. The Polish Government-in-Exile in London had not come out openly in supporting the Russian retort that it was the Germans, and not the Russians, who had murdered the flower of the Polish officer corps in the Katyn Forest. The affair of Katyn Forest has yet to be closed.

It was in Kuibyshev that we foreign correspondents suffered our first "casualty." Many Polish refugees were being harbored in camps in Soviet Central Asia, and there was much interest in foreign circles over their well-being. However, no foreign correspondent or other foreigner was permitted to visit them.

One English-speaking Pole had recently joined the Correspondents' group as representative of a British newspaper and he was greatly interested in seeing these camps first-hand and reporting on how his fellow countrymen were faring. Consequently, he applied to the Press Department of the Foreign Ministry for the necessary permission. After several weeks he received a reply in the affirmative and, in high spirits, he spread the good news among his colleagues. The necessary travel permits were supplied him soon after and he made hasty preparations to depart.

I saw him on the day of his departure and wished him well. But neither I nor any other correspondent ever saw him again. Although confirmation was impossible, it was reliably rumored that he had been arrested as he boarded the train. Another rumor had it that he was arrested en route, and still another that he had been arrested at his destination.

After the foreign colony returned to Moscow in 1943, it was reported that our Polish colleague was incarcerated in the MVD's Lubyanka prison. What his "crime" had been never became known. This, however, was the only "war casualty" among the correspondents covering the Russian front during the entire war.

At the height of the battle of Stalingrad, which was some distance down the Volga, German planes once in a while ranged over Kuibyshev, apparently on reconnaissance flights. On one such occasion a heavy bombing raid was expected, and the air-raid warning signals went into operation. So far as anybody knew, there were no public air-raid shelters in Kuibyshev; the Russians, apparently, had never expected the Germans to penetrate to anywhere near the Volga.

I contacted the Foreign Ministry Press Department by telephone and asked if any shelters were available.

The official advised us to come to the opera house so my

wife and I hurriedly made our way there through the darkness, about four blocks from where we lived. We, along with other foreigners, were directed to an elevator, which went down for about three floors, then let us out. We were then directed down a curving ramp and boarded another elevator. This one seemed to go down for at least another three floors.

After walking down a short corridor, we came out into a spacious carpeted room furnished with comfortable chairs and divans. There were smaller rooms, too, off the corridor, and there members of the diplomatic corps were playing cards, checkers or chess.

There had been no air-raid warnings before, so nobody even knew that this shelter existed. I learned that it was well stocked with food and other necessities. Subway excavating equipment had been brought from Moscow to construct this deep underground hideout. I saw only foreigners and a few important Russian officials there, so I presumed it had not been intended for ordinary Russians. My inquiries afterward supported this presumption.

From well-informed sources I learned that this deep under ground bunker had been hurried built as a shelter for top-ranking Soviet government officials—if the need arose—and for Stalin had Moscow fallen to the Germans. It was equipped with an excellent communications system, hidden ventilation installations, and was capable of withstanding a long siege.

Its location under the opera house, with an inside entrance that could be easily camouflaged, would have made its discovery extremely difficult for the Germans, certainly far more so than Hitler's rather conspicuous bunker in Berlin.

Life was becoming quite prosaic, even boring in Kuibyshev, and the most frustrated people in the city were the war correspondents who longed to be in the battle zones. The opera, of course, was excellent and many of the best theatrical stars from Moscow were now living in Kuibyshev and performing there. One could cross the Volga for swimming at a sandy beach on the other side, or merely sit around the levee and watch the boats go by.

There were also the peasant markets on the outskirts of the city, where there was brisk trading in milk, eggs, honey, meat, vegetables and a Russian tobacco called Makhorka—which I was told was made from the roots, but not the leaves, of some kind of tobacco plant. I bought a bag of this ersatz tobacco one day; it burnt like coal in my pipe, causing me to employ a glove to hold the pipe's hot bowl. But I could not complain. As I later observed, Russian soldiers were often using dried horse manure and pieces of old newspapers for rolling cigarettes in some of the front areas.

But the prosaic and lazy days on the Volga were coming to an end. Soon we would be moving on to one or the other of the theaters of hostilities.

CHAPTER XVIII

Return to Moscow

Our Wehrmacht suffered only a temporary setback.
—German soldier to the author.

THE AUTUMN OF 1941 passed into the icy grip of Russia's
first war winter and I and other war correspondents were
still rusticating in Kuibyshev on the Volga. Up until now, our
designation as war correspondent had been a misnomer. We
had protested in vain to the Russian authorities that they were
preventing us from fulfilling our duties, that we wanted to go
to the theater of hostilities. But their amazing reply was that
it was "dangerous out there, somebody might get hurt" and
that they were responsible for our safety!

We rejected this as an unacceptable answer and persisted,
reminding them that Russian war correspondents were in the
battle zones, while we were being discriminated against. I
recall reminding a Russian Foreign Ministry Official that foreign war correspondents everywhere take war risks, that no
country can be held answerable for casualties among foreign
correspondents and such dangers are part of a war correspondent's daily work.

My personal guess was that the foreign correspondents

were being kept from the scene of hostilities because the Germans were still mauling the Red Army and the Russian authorities did not want any foreign correspondents to witness and write about their continuous retreat. We were being held back, I assumed, until the Red Army had made a stand and won its first solid victory.

In retrospect, my assumption appears to have been correct. The Red Army did make a resolute stand and won a solid victory at the battle for Moscow. A powerful Russian offensive— with an early and bitter winter as an ally—had broken the siege of Moscow and the German besiegers had been forced back into retreat. Now, indeed, was the appropriate time to take foreign war correspondents into the battle zone.

Around mid-December of 1941, we were notified that we could go to the Moscow front. At long last, we were actually to become war correspondents. In the early weeks of the war, it is true, a few of the foreign correspondents had been taken on a flying tour of the Central Front and to within sound of the guns near Vitebak, but they had been whisked back to Moscow almost immediately.

The Russian authorities in Kuibyshev commandeered an ancient Polish sleeping car, a Polish porter was put aboard, a wheezy old locomotive was coupled on, and our little train was flagged off toward Moscow. The journey was to be somewhat of a battle in itself—against General Winter.

My wife had prepared enough food to last me for three days and no traveler in Russia ever goes on a journey without a few bottles of vodka. And this is doubly true in the harsh Russian winter, when vodka proves a most effective and satisfying central heating device.

Soon we were rolling along at a fairly lively pace across the vast and snow-covered steppe. On one of the coach's platforms stood a huge heater which was supposed to circulate heat through the coach by a series of pipes. The Polish porter, whose Russian was understandable only to himself, appeared to be continually stoking this heater, but no heat was circulating through the coach's compartments. There was nothing we could do about it, though I did several times ask where the heat was going. He merely shrugged his shoulders. My guess was that there was a break in the steampipe somewhere and the steam was escaping under the coach.

Darkness comes early in winter and with no heat and nothing to do, I crawled into my berth, fully clad, and went to sleep. I have always been an early riser and I awoke at seven o'clock the next morning. The train was not moving. I raised the shade but the window glass was covered with frost. I removed it from inside the pane with an old newspaper, but the glass still remained white on the outside.

Finally, I went to the platform, out of curiosity, and as I opened the door a cascade of snow crashed in on me. An aggregation of farmers from a nearby collective were digging an opening through the snow to the coach's door. Earlier in the night the train had become stalled in a cut, about five miles from the nearest station, by an all night snowstorm. The snow had piled up nearly to the roof of the coach.

The engineer had sent our porter on a distress call to a nearby farm and one of the farmers had been rushed in his troika to the station to report our plight. About two hours later, a wheezing, whining and chugging was heard up the line as a snowplow, driven by a locomotive, battled its way toward our helpless train. We were finally liberated, with the help of much picking and shovelling by the collective farmers, and were off again towards Moscow, arriving on the third day out of Kuibyshev.

We were housed in the old squat Metropole Hotel, peacetime stamping ground of foreign correspondents. Rooms were plentiful so I moved into a spacious, luxurious corner room with a European correspondent, but I soon found that a Russian winter was no respecter of luxury, especially in an unheated hotel.

I had to work in my overcoat and winter boots. In order to type, I cut off the fingertips of an old pair of gloves. But winter was deepening, and I soon moved to a smaller modest room by myself. Perhaps it would hold less cold and might be a few degrees warmer.

There were mostly new faces among the hotel employes. Two or three of the old chambermaids were still around and also the bearded and gold-braided doorman. He was an old friend and once had told me that he had held this same job during Czarist days. Apparently he was pleased to see me back, for he remarked, "See, I open the door for you with the same eagerness and courtesy as I used to do for Counts, Dukes and millionaires."

I asked what he would have done had the Germans captured Moscow.

"I would have fulfilled my duties—opened the door," he answered philosophically, and saluting.

Moscow was like a deserted city, with the feel and smell of war everywhere. It was estimated that more than half of the population had evacuated the city and the former teeming streets were almost deserted. Militiamen and MPs were on patrol throughout the city. Everybody was hungry and tense.

With their great talent for improvisation, the Russian authorities had managed to provide and stock a special food shop for the Allied foreign military mission men who had arrived in the city. The foreign correspondents were also provided with passes to this shop—besides having access to a special dining room in the Metropole Hotel. This meant that I had two sources of obtaining food and drink.

One of my first concerns was the fate of my old neighbors, Pavel Pavlevich and his family. I had also some thoughts about Catherine Pushkin. Going out to the apartment building where I had lived, I found the building completely empty, the windows all blown out and the main entrance padlocked. Through inquiries nearby, I managed to locate the caretaker.

He was a new man, but lived in the same neighborhood. He recognized me and let me into the building.

I found my apartment in complete disarray. Everything of any value that I had left behind was missing. When I gave the caretaker an inquisitive look, he shrugged.

"The whole building was looted when the roar of German guns got loud. Your old caretaker got away with the first loot."

I learned that many looters, some of them deserters from the front, had been shot on sight all over the city during the panicky and chaotic days of late October and in November.

(I recall that at the end of the war in 1945, I saw an act of unpardonable ingratitude being attempted in front of my apartment building, which had been repaired and back into which I had moved. Upon returning from downtown one summer day, two Jeeps were parked in the courtyard in front of the main entrance to the building. I saw two Red Army soldiers wiping away on the hoods of the Jeeps and presumed they were removing dust. But when I approached and stood beside the Jeeps, to my amazement I found them trying to scrub "U.S.A." markings off with gasoline-soaked rags! I doubted that they were doing this of their own volition; it was possible they were carrying out an order.)

The new caretaker pointed out the building nearby into which Pavel Pavlevich and his family had moved. He and his wife and son were at home and they welcomed me as if I had been a member of their family. They told me of some of the privations they had experienced in the besieged city—no heat, scarcity of food, sporadic air raids, etc. But they said they had no intention of leaving Moscow.

Pavel's wife apologized for not having anything to put on the table, not even tea. I was not surprised—they were but one hungry family in a city of hungry people. I asked Pavel and his son to come to my hotel on the following evening. In the meantime, I visited the special food shop and obtained a large basketful of foodstuffs.

With a promptness unusual for Russians, Pavel and his six-teen-year-old son arrived at the appointed hour. I then phoned for a waiter to bring up the one meal I was allowed and gave it to my guests. They devoured it with undisguised gusto.

When my good friends were ready to leave, I handed them the basket of food. Pavel's thanks were profuse and he offered to reimburse me, but I refused to accept any payment. He then insisted that I come to his house the next day, saying that his wife would prepare a feast and he wanted me there to share it.

My urge to be a Good Samaritan took me next day to the apartment house in which my wife had lived as a child. Only one family, who knew me well, remained in the building. The husband was away at the front but his wife and their daughter Elena welcomed me.

The wife plied me with questions about Marie Petrovna, for she had known my wife since she was born. Nothing had been heard from her husband since he left for the front that summer and she did not know whether he was dead or alive. She, too, had nothing to offer me, and when hospitable Russians have nothing to offer a guest, then one knows that the cupboard is bare.

"Come to my hotel tomorrow evening, please," I said. "I'll have something for you."

The older woman arrived with her red-haired daughter Elena promptly at the appointed hour and I missed another hot meal that evening. I had again gone to the special food shop and had a basket of food ready for them.

"Have you a bathroom?" Elena's mother asked.

I arose and opened the bathroom door.

"If you will please excuse us, we haven't had a good hot bath for some time. Could Elena and I come tomorrow and use your bathroom?"

"Of course," I answered. "I expect to be back at the hotel by six o'clock."

Mother and daughter came on time the next evening, too, and I told them, "It's all yours. I am going to take a stroll through Red Square and along the Moscow River embankment. I'll return in about an hour."

The evening of the next day I went to look for my old and good friend, Catherine Pushkin. I found her living at the same place. When I arrived, she and three women neighbors were playing Ochko (a popular Russian card game) by the light of an oil lamp. Catherine was happy to see me—after four years —and introduced me to her guests as "My old and dear American friend."

I asked why the women had not evacuated the besieged city.

"What for?" one of them answered, with typical Russian fatalism. "We had nowhere to go. Better to freeze or starve in Moscow than out in the frozen steppe."

Catherine apologized for having nothing to offer me in the way of food and drink.

"Could you find a boy in the building to run an errand?" I asked.

One of the women excused herself and quickly returned with her fifteen-year-old son. I asked Catherine to make a list of what she needed, gave my pass to the boy and told him the address of the special food shop.

"Oleg, I know that the blackout is on and nobody is supposed to be on the streets after dark," I told him. "If you are stopped by the militia or an MP, just show him my pass. I think that will take care of everything."

He was off in a jiffy, returning an hour later with a basketful of food and a few bottles of vodka. We soon had a little ball. I left for my hotel, five blocks away, at about eleven o'clock hoping that I too could run the blackout blockade. I moved along close to the walls of buildings, but no sooner had I turned the corner of Gorky Street and Okhotny Road, than a flashlight was directed at my face.

I tried to explain to the two militiamen why I was on the

street at that time of night, in violation of the blackout rules. But orders were orders, and one of them escorted me to a police station five blocks away, just off Pushkin Street. It was not considered a crime to be caught on the street during a blackout; violators were merely taken to the nearest police station, where they had to remain until daybreak.

When I arrived at the station, a number of violators were sleeping on the floor and on benches. The militia chief took a surprised look at me and scratched his chin.

"Gospodin (Sir), I am afraid it would be very uncomfortable for you to have to spend the night here. Where do you live?"

When I told him I lived at the Metropole Hotel, he ordered the militiaman who had brought me in to escort me to the hotel and make certain to confirm that I actually lived there.

Arriving at the hotel, I tapped on the plate-glass door. The night watchman peeped out from behind the black curtain and when he unlocked the door the militiaman asked, "Does this Gospodin live here?"

"Sure, I know him," the doorman answered.

The militiaman saluted and marched away into the blackout.

The next day I moved into the battle zone west of Moscow. Snow lay heavy on the ground; the cold was intense. But I was well protected by my fur-lined overcoat, fur cap pulled down over my ears and knee-high valenkis on my feet. The old Russian sedan, driven by a Russian chauffeur, bounced along over the route where only a few days previously bitter and decisive battles had been fought.

My first stop was Borodino, the famous village battlefield where, in 1812, Napoleon and his Grand Army had defeated Russian Field Marshal Mikhail Kutuzov, enabling Napoleon to smash ahead and capture Moscow. The Germans, too, had defeated the Russians at Borodino and advanced on Moscow, a defeat that was a heavy blow to Russian national pride. But, unlike Napoleon, the Germans lost the battle for Moscow.

The ferociousness of the fighting in this area was attested to by limbless trees, the trunks shattered or scarred by ricocheting shells and bullets. Here and there I saw bayonets of rifles projecting above the snow—some the German knife type and others the long, slender sort used by the Russians. They now stood as markers where attacker and defender had fallen in mortal combat, and would remain immured under the thick canopy of snow until uncovered by the spring thaws.

In one snowy field a battery of German long-range guns stood abandoned by the road, their frost-covered barrels pointing threateningly in the direction of Moscow. The Germans had planned on shelling the city, with the Kremlin a prime target. But the Red Army's counterattack had been so swift and powerful that the Germans found neither time to fire the guns nor to move them away. There they stood, forsaken and forlorn, with the snow piled up to the hubs of their wheels.

In the village of Borodino I met my first German war prisoners—and a sorry sight they were. Their noses were frozen and swollen, looking not unlike small eggplants. They had Russian peasant shawls wrapped around their heads and necks. On their feet they wore Russian valenkis.

Hitler had expected to defeat Russia during the summer months and had not prepared his army for winter combat. His intuition had told him that before winter fell, his soldiers would already be comfortably billeted in Moscow and other Russian cities. But Russian resistance had been unexpectedly stubborn and winter had caught the Germans without heavy winter clothing and to protect themselves from the merciless Russian winter, they had to loot winter clothes from Russian peasants.

This first confrontation began with a hitch. Several of the German prisoners knew English, but the Russian officer in charge would permit no direct questions to be asked or answered. He demanded that questions be directed to an interpreter who would translate the questions into German and relay the answers in English. Apparently, the only reason for this round-about question-and-answer method was that the Russians wanted to "process" the data.

Despite their bedraggled condition, the Germans tried to maintain a soldierly bearing—even a semblance of hauteur. While admitting that the German Army had suffered a setback in the battle for Moscow, none would admit the possibility of Germany ultimately losing the war.

Later I visited a barracks some distance farther on where other German prisoners were housed. There were rows of iron cots in the rooms, which were heated, and the Russian authorities appeared to be observing all the Geneva Convention rules for the treatment of war prisoners.

All the Germans housed here appeared to be young and strapping, no doubt members of the Hitlerjugend youth organization. I was surprised at how well most of them spoke English. When I managed to be alone with two of them in one of the rooms for a moment, I asked why they spoke English so well.

"We were trained for the invasion of England," one of them answered. "We were stationed along the English Channel, but when things got so hot on the Eastern front, we were hurriedly transferred to Russia."

"Do you still feel like Herrenvolk, after the beating you suffered in the battle for Moscow?" I asked.

With Nazi arrogance one of them answered, "Our Wehrmacht suffered only a temporary setback. We shall return and take Moscow."

"When?"

"Our Fueher will decide that," he answered, standing as if at attention for inspection by his commanding officer.

Shortly before Christmas, I visited the town of Nara-Fominsk, about twenty-five miles southwest of Moscow, which the Russian 33rd and 43rd armies had recently re-captured. The German command had been so cocksure of holding Nara-

Fominsk that they had made extensive preparations for a big Christmas ball. A large hall had been decorated with colored streamers, stocks of wines and vodka made ready and all the young women in the neighborhood rounded up for a night of pleasure.

Then the Red Army made a surprising, crushing attack on December 18th and the Germans made a panicky retreat into the snowy waste. I went into a room on the second floor of a building on the main street and found a German General's coat and trousers draped over the back of a chair beside the bed. He had apparently decamped hurriedly and pantless in his staff car. I also found an item of feminine wear on a table.

Other battle zones in the northern and southern sectors of Moscow came under my observation during the next few weeks. Everywhere the bitter and bloody fighting had left its mark of destruction—crushed buildings and houses, denuded trees, shell holes, smashed tanks and other vehicles.

And alongside the roads I saw copses of white crosses, almost indiscernible in the snow. Under these markers lay thousands of Hanses and Fritzes—Hitler's supermen sent on his Lebensraum Drang noch Osten. All they had gained was possession of six feet of Russian soil. One of the oddest aspects of my battle zone travels, not only around Moscow but elsewhere, was that I never saw a Russian war cemetery. Were dead Russian soldiers collected from the battlefield and cremated or buried in hidden mass graves? I was unable to find an answer to this question.

At long last, I was beginning to get the feel and smell and to witness at first hand the repulsiveness and destructiveness of war. I remembered that fine balanced sentence: "In peace, sons bury their fathers; in war, fathers bury their sons."

But this was only the beginning—three and one-half years of war's fury and anguish still lay ahead of me in Russia and the Crimea.

CHAPTER XIX

Murder in the Katyn Forest

Murder Will Out
—Cervantes—Don Quixote

AFTER I CAME BACK from the wars in Russia friends asked me what was the most ghastly and shocking sight I saw during a conflict that was singularly savage. Unhesitatingly, my answer has been: My visit to the Katyn Forest.

I happen to be one of the few foreigners, and the only Negro, to have visited the scene of the macabre murder of some eleven thousand Polish army officers, and I still have vivid memories of the scene of that savage slaughter in the dreamy spruce forest of Katyn near Smolensk.

I first heard of the Katyn Forest affair not from Russian sources, but from a German radio announcement on April 13, 1943. A mass grave containing the bodies of thousands of Polish officers had been discovered in the Katyn Forest, Berlin disclosed, and they accused Russia of having committed this gruesome crime.

Radio Moscow immediately retorted vehemently that the German charge was a "vile fabrication." As could have been expected, the Russian authorities loudly and heatedly accused the Germans of having committed the atrocity themselves.

Russia was an ally of the West at the time and had won deep admiration for her heroic and stubborn struggle against her one-time ally, Nazi Germany. Besides, the Germans had already committed so many atrocities in Europe and Russia that I, along with other correspondents in Russia, was inclined to disbelieve the German charge. Thus there was an overwhelming inclination to place the guilt on the Germans. One of my foreign diplomatic friends called the German exposé "a masterpiece of Goebbelsian propaganda."

With quick ingeniousness, Hitler ordered an on-the-spot investigation early in 1943, inviting non-German experts in pathology, criminology, forensic medicine, law and related professions from twelve countries to join in the investigation.

The findings of this International Medical Commission, signed by twelve international experts after they had completed their exhaustive investigation of hundreds of bodies, were unanimous in affirming that the victims had been dead and buried since the spring of 1940—that is, more than one year before the Germans occupied the Katyn Forest.

In September, 1943, the Red Army recaptured Smolensk and the Katyn Forest from the Germans, and the Kremlin, in high dudgeon ever since the German accusation of a few months earlier, quickly ordered its own investigation. A Special Soviet Commission, under the direction of Dr. N. N. Burdenko, noted Russian doctor, was organized to carry out its own post-mortem.

Dr. Burdenko was appointed personally by Stalin to head the Soviet investigating team. Just when these all-Russian investigators arrived in the Katyn Forest and began their unpleasant task was not revealed. But with the stage well set in advance, the Kremlin later found it expedient to invite a group of Allied war correspondents stationed on the German-Russian front to visit the Katyn Forest and observe the activities of the Russian investigators. This, however, was more than four months after recapture of the Katyn Forest by the Red Army.

What had been happening at the site of the slaughter during the intervening months? Why was the invitation to the Allied correspondents issued only after a certain amount of preliminary work had been carried out? Those were questions that we correspondents pondered at the time.

Before proceeding to the Katyn Forest, I should like to relate the Kremlin's reaction to the exposure of the crime as I saw it. When Berlin had exposed the atrocity in 1943, Stalin and his Kremlin associates—Khrushchev, Molotov, Beria, Bulganin, Mikoyan, Malenkov and others—were known to have been filled with rage over this tremendous propaganda scoop by Hitler and Goebbels. Quick counter-measures had to be taken, and the London Polish Government-in-Exile became the first target of the Kremlin's fury.

It so happened that the shocked London Polish Government, upon learning of the atrocity, had immediately invited the International Red Cross to conduct a neutral and impartial on the spot investigation. The International Red Cross was willing to undertake the grisly talks, but suggested cooperation by the three countries directly involved—Germany, Poland and Russia. Germany and Poland consented, but Russia reacted violently against such a suggestion.

Vyacheslav Molotov, then Soviet Foreign Minister, immediately called the discovery merely "an archeological remains." *Pravda* (April 19, 1943) retorted that such an investigation was unnecessary because "something that never happened cannot be investigated." The Soviet Government angrily denounced the London Polish Government as "Nazi collaborators."

The Kremlin followed this up by immediately breaking off diplomatic relations (April 26, 1943) with the London Polish Government. Polish Ambassador Tadeuesz Romer and his staff were at once informed that they were *persona non grata*.

It appeared that *lese majesty* had been committed by the London Poles.

When I visited the Polish Embassy in Kuibyshev (all foreign diplomatic missions were still located in Kuibyshev), I could see by the hasty packing activities that the now unwelcome Polish Embassy was making every effort to comply with the Kremlin's order. In addition, the resurgent Polish Army, then being organized and trained near Kuibyshev by General Wladyslaw Sikorski, was also being readied to leave Russia.

Thus there was great expectation among the Allied correspondents when, in mid-January, 1944, the Press Department of the Soviet Ministry of Foreign Affairs announced a trip to the Katyn Forest.

Our train of sleepers and a diner, well-stocked with food and the perennial vodka, began to crawl westwards toward Smolensk through litters of war wreckage, both Russian and German. Some of the heaviest battles during the German Wehrmacht's dash eastward toward Moscow at the start of the war had been along this line. Here we had observed in the summer of 1941 whole Russian armies were being surrounded, surrendering, or fleeing in panic from Hitler's determined juggernaut. Here death and destruction had reigned supreme during the early months of the war. This way Napoleon had also come in 1812—and fled with the remnants of his polyglot army.

Arriving at battered Smolensk, we were transferred to American Jeeps for the ten-mile drive to the Katyn Forest. I was not too sure we would arrive there alive, because our Russian chauffeurs would have been more at home on the Indianapolis Speedway than on this loose-gravel road. In little or no time, however, we were pulling off into the deathly silence of the snow-covered, barbed-wire-enclosed Katyn Forest.

Leaping out of my Jeep before it had come to a full stop, I found myself staring down into a huge open pit. Looking more closely, I saw bodies closely stacked twelve deep, one on top of

another. Red Army soldiers were picking and digging and pry-
ing the stiff, fully-clad corpses from the stacks. Other Red
Army stretcher bearers were bringing their cold and stark
loads up an earthern ramp out of this vast grave.

An aura of death hung over the whole area. Here, indeed, I
stood awe-struck in the presence of one of the most cold-
blooded crimes of the war. Ambassador W. Averill Harriman's
daughter, Kathleen, who stood alongside me, turned as if wanting to say something, but she merely moaned and choked.
Though she was not a correspondent, she had been permitted
to make the trip with us.

After circling the rim of this corpse-packed pit several times,
with my nostrils filled with the dull and musty smell of death
—slightly alleviated by the fact that it was wintertime—I
moved from the nauseating sight to a level field a few yards
away.

Here, laid out in long rows, their taut and darkened faces
open to the wintry sky, were hundreds of bodies of Polish
officers in full uniform and with their boots still on. Their
uniforms and overcoats were winter issue and along with their
boots, did not seem to have had much hard wear. I noticed
that some hands were tied with rope, others with wire.

Anyone who has been on a battlefield moves nonchalantly
among the corpses of soldiers killed in action. One has the feeling that they had died in the line of duty, in the heat of battle
where it was to kill or be killed. But I was never so deeply
touched on any battlefield as I was by this host of corpses of
Polish officers who had been dug out of that vast pit.

In defending their country against heavy odds from Hitler's
army from the West, they had been compelled to retreat eastwards into conflict with Stalin's Red Army attacking from the
East—ending up in this mass grave in the Katyn Forest. At
whose order and by whose hands?

Although my tour of this forest of slaughter and destruction
had only begun, it was already obvious that an appreciable

amount of preliminary work had already been done. The area already dug open by physical hand labor and the hundreds of bodies exhumed and laid out in the field most certainly had required many days of work. Autopsy by the Soviet Special (Medical) Commission was well advanced in the large tent that had been erected at the site.

I jotted down a few questions in my notebook. Why had no foreign newsmen been invited to be present when the opening of the grave began? Why had we not been permitted to be present when the first autopsies were being performed? Why had Stalin not invited any Allied or neutral experts to join the Soviet Investigating team? Why had the spruce saplings that had been removed from on top of the grave grown to a height indicating that they had been planted three or four years earlier?

Turning from the gruesome sea of corpses, I went into the large tent where autopsies were being performed. This sight was even more macabre. Members of the Soviet Investigating team, around improvised tables, were sawing off the tops of skulls and removing brains, ripping open stomachs and pulling out entrails and hearts.

The experts and their assistants were hardly communicative. However, one doctor did point out to me a bullet hole at the base of the skull of the corpse he was examining, and remarked that similar bullet holes had been found in the skulls of other corpses.

A hot pot-bellied stove in the tent had caused the air to become filled with the odor of decaying bodies. This, together with the sight of the sawing and ripping, made me so nauseated that I could stand it no longer, so I made my way to the outside air.

As I pulled back the flap of this chamber of horrors, I ran head-on into old Dr. Burdenko, whom I had met in Moscow during pre-war days. He smiled over our near head-on collision and we shook hands. I asked Dr. Burdenko a few unprovocative questions, since America and Russia were still allies in a struggle for survival against Hitler Germany. But he proved uncommunicative too, his only answer being that an official report would be issued when they had completed their work.

From Dr. Burdenko's taciturn reference to the "official report," I gained the impression that he had been sent to do a job, to "prove something." However, I suspected that buried in that magnificent head, that fine old pre-Revolution doctor of distinction and integrity had thoughts he dared not express. (Incidentally, Dr. Burdenko was deaf but he was an expert lip reader.)

There were many questions I could, with good reason and justification, have asked Dr. Burdenko. Why were the officers clad in overcoats and winter issue when Stalin had declared categorically that they were murdered by the Nazis during the balmy days of August and September? Or why did their boots and uniforms show so little signs of wear if, as the Kremlin claimed, they had been working as Russian prisoners from 1939 until their capture by the Germans in 1941?

Why was the neutral International Red Cross not permitted to make an impartial investigation, as was proposed by the London Polish Government *and* the German Government? Why had no neutral or allied experts been invited to work with the Soviet experts during the present exhumation and autopsies? Why had the Poles, if left unguarded in their camp after the Russian guards had fled at the appearance of the Germans, not fled also? And if, as the Kremlin claimed, no transport facilities were available, why had the Polish officers not been marched to the rear on foot? But I did not ask these questions.

Seeing a large table a short distance away, I moved over to see what was on exhibition. On the table were some of the personal belongings of the dead Polish officers, said to have been found on their persons. Here were cigarette lighters, holders and cases, Polish zlotys, snapshots of wives and children, mothers and sweethearts, fathers, sisters, brothers, relatives, army identification tickets, medals, and emblems.

Most intriguing were the many letters and post cards from home said to have been found in the murdered officers' pockets. I could not read Polish, but I could read dates. And a Red Army officer was noticeably helpful in calling my attention to them, all of which were later than July, 1941.

But, I thought, this proved nothing. The letters and post cards could have been easily faked to prove that the men were still alive when Germany attacked Russia and captured the camps in western Russia in which the Polish officers were being held prisoners.

As I wandered about the site, a Russian in black padded winter overcoat, high black leather boots and round black fur cap opened his right hand, revealing several empty cartridge casings. "German made," he said, pointing to the German markings around the primer holes.

"Yes, German made," I answered, purposely keeping any doubts suppressed.

But the letterings on cartridge cases, like the dates on the letters and post cards, proved nothing. It was known to informed foreigners that a German firm had for many years supplied ammunition to Russia, Poland and the three formerly independent Baltic states of Lithuania, Latvia and Esthonia, all three of which were incorporated into the Soviet Union in 1940.

This ammunition was known to be of a standard type that could be used in many different types of small-arms weapons. It was obvious that the ammunition had been made in Germany, but this did not prove who had used it to blast holes through the skulls of the Polish officers exhumed in the Katyn Forest.

The ammunition could have been captured from the German Army; it could have been taken over from the Baltic states incorporated into the Soviet Union; it could have been from the pre-war ammunition German firms exported to Russia. Indeed, the ammunition might have been from weapons taken from the slain Polish officers themselves.

As afterthoughts induced by post-war events, other questions have arisen in my mind. I shall mention only two of them here.

Under the terms of the London Agreement of 1945, Russia was given the right to supervise, investigate and prosecute war crimes committed on her territory. The Nuremberg Trials certainly presented Russia with a splendid opportunity to prove her claim that the Nazis were guilty of the Katyn Forest slaughter. Yet, the Soviet Prosecutor failed to press the Katyn Forest case at Nuremberg. Strangely enough, it was the lack of zeal on the part of the Soviet Prosecutor that caused the Nuremberg Tribunal not to pursue the Katyn Forest affair.

In the fall of 1951 the Congress of the United States established a special committee, under the chairmanship of Indiana Representative Raymond Madden, to investigate fully the Katyn Forest massacre. This committee politely invited the Soviet government to cooperate by submitting factual evidence connected with the Katyn Forest crime.

But the Kremlin categorically and heatedly rejected the invitation as an insult. Instead, the Soviet government launched an intensive, slanderous campaign against the committee and its activities. Here again, in my opinion, the Kremlin bungled an excellent opportunity of producing, if it could, convincing proof of German guilt.

Perhaps the world will one day learn the indisputable answer to this wartime mystery, this crime against humanity. I do not presume to know that answer. I have merely related my own experience in the Katyn Forest and certain other matters having direct connections with the Katyn Forest affair.

CHAPTER XX

Slaughter in the Crimea

War is Hell
—Attributed to
General William T. Sherman

O VER THE PEACE-TIME YEARS, I had fallen deeply in love
with the lush and lovely Crimea, that irregular quad-
rangle-shaped peninsula jutting out into the Black Sea toward
Turkey. My happiest vacations had been spent there and I
even had slept in one of the fifty rooms of the white granite,
Italian renaissance Livadia Palace, former summer residence
of Czar Nicholas II, where President Roosevelt was later
housed at the time of the Yalta Conference, in February of
1945.

I had reveled in soft sub-tropical summers, with vineyards
stretching for miles in every direction, as the Black Sea breakers pounded the rocky shore like the intermitten roll of bass
drums. This shore in ancient times had seen Roman and Turkish galleys oared over the dark-blue waters by black galley
slaves. Dusky Tartar maidens had added their feminine allure
to my pleasure there.

The Crimea had been for me an idyllic place. Now I was
returning to this lovely land in another mood. It was high sum-

mer of 1944. Bitter fighting had been raging between the Russians and units of von Manstein's 11th Army, supported by Romanian units. I could understand why the Nazis did not wish to relax their grip on this pearl of the Black Sea; I could as readily understand why the Russians were determined to re-occupy it.

My plane put down at Simferopol, the Crimean capital, which is in the center of the peninsula. I transferred there to an American Jeep for the dash through the Crimean Mountains to Yalta, which I found little damaged. I had hoped to quench my thirst at the nearby famous Imperial Massandra Wine Cellars, which had held over two million bottles of choice wines. But the Germans and Romanians apparently had been thirsty too, for I was told that the great cellars were now empty.

I could not tarry in Yalta, for my destination was Sevastopol. But looking up at the sun-drenched mountains back of Yalta, I recalled with nostalgia that during one of my peace-time visits I had hiked in those pristine mountains with a dusky, black-haired, black-eyed Tartar girl named Liza, and tarried with her in an ancient and abandoned Armenian church.

My Jeep labored its way up the mountain road out of Yalta, and soon before me stood lovely Livadia Palace, high on a cliff overlooking the Black Sea. On one of my peace-time visits here I had been told that the room to which I had been assigned was once occupied by Rasputin—with a connecting door to the Czarina's apartments.

After a few hours of hard driving, my car skirted Balaklava, where during the Crimean War the Light Brigade, celebrated by Tennyson, had charged into the valley of death. A short distance away lay Sevastopol, where I was to find that death and destruction had had a field day every day for the past eight long months.

I did much walking in the fields around Sevastopol. The

fighting here had been savage. Hundreds of rotting Romanian cavalry horses, swollen to balloon size, littered the fields. The stench of decaying horse carcasses and human corpses was nauseating, made increasingly so by the fact that it was hot summertime. I regretted that I had not brought some cotton to plug my nostrils. I felt that if I had kicked the bloated belly of one of the horses, it would have burst in my face. But I had been warned by a Russian officer not to touch anything—the Germans might have left any object mined.

The fields were littered with German occupation money which the gentle winds swirled about like confetti. The currency, now worthless, was good only as souvenirs, so I picked up a few bills for this purpose.

Von Manstein's army had burst into the Crimea across the narrow Ishun neck of land connecting the Crimea with the mainland. Russian military authorities had never been able to conceive of the possibility of an attack by land and had heavily fortified the city to withstand an assault only from the sea. In other words, heavy coastal batteries had been built to face the sea, but very little attention had been devoted to defenses on the land side.

German intelligence, fully aware of this defensive weakness, launched their land drive against the city's virtually exposed rear and sent the Russian land forces reeling back into Sevastopol, with their backs to the sea. Thus they became reinforcements for Vice Admiral Oktyabrsky, whose naval forces had been charged with the defense of the City. At this point Oktyabrsky had been named Supreme Commander over all Russian units in the besieged city.

Although the Russians paid a terrible price for this military shortsightedness, it must be admitted that their stubbornly holding out at Sevastopol undoubtedly tied down a powerful German army that might have been transferred to Stalingrad or directed toward the Caucasus Mountains and Russia's vital oilfields. The long and bloody contest brought to the Crimea such slaughter as it had not seen since the Crimean War of 1854–56.

When the Russians began their counterattack to drive the enemy out of the Crimea, thousands of Germans and Romanians had been slaughtered in the environs of Sevastopol. Surviving units found themselves pressed back and trapped on the Chersones Cape between the Red Army and the Black Sea. (The Russians had found themselves in this same predicament when the Germans captured the city in 1942.) Too, there must have been an appreciable depreciation of morale after the news of the German disaster at Stalingrad.

I moved onto the cape where thousands of dead German and Romanian, mostly Romanian, soldiers and horses had been driven off the cliffs to the sandy beach below. The breakers were still heaving up the corpses of men and carcasses of horses onto a wide expanse of the beach. As I stood looking down on this horrendous sight, I gained a fuller understanding of the meaning of the word retribution.

There were conflicting reports on how the Germans and Romanians had managed to get themselves in such a predicament. One said they had been driven from the cliff into the sea by the merciless attack of the Russians. Another claimed they had tried to escape on self-propelled barges across the sea to Romania, but that Russian planes and warships had sunk the barges.

This latter version was most likely the true one.

Sevastopol, when I entered it, remained only a name and a huge mass of rubble, where streets had been now were only piles of stone and bricks. The Germans had paid a heavy price for the capture of this empty shell, turned into its present state by many months of shelling and bombing by their own artillery and planes. But the Russians had paid a still more horrible price for defending the city.

I moved through the jagged and tottering walls of what had once been buildings. A Russian war correspondent, Boris

Voyetekov, who was in the city during the siege, told me that German attrition had been so devastating that only about one hundred Russian defenders remained when the city finally fell.

Sevastopol was the most thoroughly destroyed city in Russia, not excepting Stalingrad. I was now looking at the city just as President Roosevelt was to see it when he visited Sevastopol after the Yalta Conference early in 1945—scorched and scarred like a forest through which fire had swept.

It was a great mental relief for me to leave Sevastopol—such devastation can be terribly depressing—and I hastened to get away from it. On my way back to Simferopol, where the plane was waiting to fly me back to Moscow, my car passed through Bakhchisarai (Palace of Gardens), a quiet and slumbering town nestling in orchards in a narrow valley along the small Tchuryuk-Su River. Here in the 15th century the Khans of the Crimea had begun their reign.

In the courtyard of the Khans' palace had stood the famous Fountain of Tears, built by Krim-Girai Khan of gilded white marble in honor of Dilara-Biketch, his favorite wife. And it was of this self-same fountain that Pushkin later sang in his well-known poem, *The Fountain of Bakhchisarai*.

During the flight back to Moscow, my plane flew over the great Dneiper Hydroelectric Power Station, which American know-how and machinery had produced for Stalin during his First Five Year Plan. I looked down on a gaping break in the great dam across the Dneiper River through which water was rushing in torrents.

Early in the war I had heard Stalin announce his scorched earth policy, which assured the Russian people that the great power installation had been wrecked and made useless for the Germans. But after the Germans retreated later in the war and the station fell back into Russian hands, Stalin accused the Germans as the vandals who had wrecked the installation.

War produces mass death and mass devastation. It also produces deceit, deception and downright lies.

CHAPTER XXI

The Man from Kolyma

The U.S.S.R. affords the right of asylum to foreign citizens persecuted for defending the interests of the working people . . .
—Article 129, Soviet Constitution

IT HAPPENED that I was the only Negro journalist ever stationed in Russia. I was also the only Negro war correspondent on the Russian-German front, and if it can be carried even a bit further, I was the first Negro to be accredited a war correspondent. This was not a calculated achievement, I had just happened to be on the scene when the shooting started and all of the civilian correspondents were placed on war footing. Early in 1944 I joined the staff of the *Associated Press,* Moscow Bureau, by invitation and with approval from the New York office and on a salaried basis. Henry Cassidy, the Chief of the AP Moscow Bureau, returned to New York in May, 1944, and from that time on Eddy Gilmore and I were the American team in the AP Bureau.

In addition to the American staff—Gilmore and myself— five Russians worked for the Bureau—Lida and Elena, two lovely Russian secretaries; a middle-aged woman and a boy who acted as our messengers, rushing cables to the Foreign Ministry for clearance and afterwards to the Telegraph Office; and a Russian man who drove the Bureau car.

The Metropole, where the Associated Press as well as the *United Press, Reuters,* the *New York Times, Herald Tribune, London Times,* and so on, all had their offices, was then the leading hotel in Moscow. It was right in the center of the city, across the square from the Bolshoi Theater. These offices were actually ordinary hotel rooms, with a bath and toilet, and AP occupied a suite of two down near the end of a long hall on the second floor. It was on the east side of the building and from my desk I could look out and see the big green and forbidding headquarters building of the MVD, which also housed the notorious Lubyanka prison. As a rule, I opened the Bureau every morning around seven o'clock, and this was always the first sight that greeted me. Fortunately I never got a better, "inside" view of that evil place.

One midday in late 1944 the ringing telephone interrupted my typing in the Bureau office. I expected it to be a routine call from one of the Foreign Ministry censors about a story we had sent over for clearance or an invitation to a cocktail party from some fellow foreigner. But the call turned out to be far more unusual and intriguing.

"I'd like to speak with the Chief of Bureau," the caller asked in an American-English accent. I told him that the Chief, Eddy Gilmore, was away.

"Who is in charge at the moment?" he asked. I explained that I was.

"Then I must see you as quickly as possible."

"Come on up," I answered.

"Could we meet at some other place?" he asked.

This suggestion, quite naturally, aroused my journalistic curiosity. It was commonly known in foreign circles that Secret Police spies were always loitering in the Metropole lobby. They were also said to be planted among the hotel employes.

"I am going to the post office in a few minutes," I suggested. "Suppose we meet there?"

He agreed, and then there arose the question of recognition. A simple solution was decided; he was to stand near the block of post office boxes and the person who opened a certain box number would be me. I could have given him a quicker method of identifying me. I did not.

When I entered the post office I saw near the boxes a heavy-set, sallow-complexioned man in coarse though presentable overcoat, a fur cap and black valenkis, the hard felt typical Russian knee-high winter boots. As I opened my box, he sidled toward me.

"AP?"

Upon my replying in the affirmative, he remarked, "Oh, you are a colored man. I had many colored friends in America."

He pushed a ham-like hand into mine. His grip was like a vise and his hand was as calloused as a stevedore's. His hunted look and obvious uneasiness convinced me that he was nervous.

"Could we go some other place and talk?" he asked.

I suggested taking different subway trains to suburban Sokolniki Park. Within thirty minutes we were seated on a bench in the park.

First of all, I wanted to know who he was, where he came from and why had he telephoned the *Associated Press* Bureau. He began telling his story, which if true, was utterly fascinating. I shall call him Mr. K.

Back in 1930, Mr. K began, he had been active in the labor movement in California. Police harassment, he said, had made him decide to leave America for Russia, where asylum was offered to any foreigners persecuted for his working class activity in any capitalist country. He had arrived in Moscow in 1930 and joined the sizable and polyglot colony of so-called "political immigrants" from several countries, including the United States.

"Were you a member of the American Communist Party?" I interposed.

He declared he had never been a Communist Party member, but admitted that he had then been in sympathy with most Communist ideals and party programs.

Several months after his arrival in Russia, he continued, he and several other fellow "political immigrants," Communist and non-communist alike, had become dissatisfied with their living conditions and with many other things they had not expected to find in the "Fatherland of the toiling masses and the home of the dictatorship of the proletariat."

They had made the fatal mistake of openly expressing their discontent and shortly afterwards all were arrested as "class hostile elements," in need of "corrective re-education." He was sent to a concentration camp in the White Sea area and later was transferred to Kolyma, in the Russian Sub-Arctic northeast. There he had remained ever since—a total of fourteen years of "corrective" training in one of Stalin's most notorious slave labor camps.

"How did you manage to escape?" I asked.

Mr. K had the war to thank for his flight to his present uneasy freedom. With Russia still sorely in need of every ablebodied man, volunteers were recruited at his camp. He had volunteered, but escaped from the train in the Ural Mountains. It had taken him six weeks to reach Moscow, hiding in the daytime and hooking rides on trains at night.

The story of his flight recalled the Underground Railway of pre-Civil War days in America. He stated that there existed an "underground railway" in Siberia, although "traffic" was light and "passengers" rare. Prisoners fortunate enough to escape, and who in some way learned where the "stations" were, could always find a temporary hideout and food. The "station masters," he claimed, were old Russian settlers, many of whom themselves had been exiled to Siberia during Czarist days or the early years of the Communist regime.

Upon reaching European Russia, the escapee's lot became both easier and more difficult. He could, by hook or crook, obtain forged documents and without too great difficulty merge with the local population; on the other hand, there were more Secret Police agents to evade.

An old Russian woman, he said, had taken him into her basement quarters in Moscow. Her own husband had been banished to the Siberian tundra several years previously and had never been heard of since. Mr. K said he had obtained her address while en route and hinted obliquely that she too was a Moscow "underground stationmaster."

With a show of deep emotion, Mr. K told me of the inhumanity, brutality and horrors of life in a Kolyma slave labor camp. I have never heard or read of anything comparable, not even on a southern chain gang. But the same dreadful story has been told and re-told so often, that its repetition here would be redundant and add nothing new to the grim picture.

However, one of the things he told me has never, to my knowledge, been made known elsewhere and deserves mention. Mr. K said he had seen black men in Kolyma. This, naturally, whetted my interest. Immediately, I wanted to know if these black slave laborers were from America.

"The men that I saw definitely were not from the States," he said. "They were not the American Negro type. Physically, they were Africans. Some of them spoke fairly good English, but with a British or foreign accent. Many did not know English at all."

"How had they landed in Kolyma?" I asked.

"As far as I was able to learn, some were 'political immigrants' like me and some had been brought to Russia to study in Communist revolutionary schools. I suppose they had become disillusioned and expressed their disillusionment too openly, then had been charged with 'ideological deviationism' or 'violators of discipline.' So they were being given 'corrective rehabilitation' in Kolyma."

"Now, why did you telephone the *Associated Press*?" I asked.

Mr. K had a plausible explanation. Back in 1930, he said, he was acquainted with the then Chief of the AP Moscow Bureau. "I knew he would hardly still be in Moscow, but I had to contact somebody. And the AP was the only place I could think of."

With the hour becoming late, we decided to end our meeting. Mr. K said he would like to see me again within two days, but I advised him against telephoning, because telephones, especially those of foreign newsmen, were known to be tapped. We, therefore, arranged a time and place in advance.

At this meeting, which took place in the Central Park of Culture and Rest, Mr. K said he was anxious to sell a story about himself and his life in Kolyma to the *Associated Press* or to some other wire service for American dollars. I told him that I did not think the AP was in the market for such material. I told him that some American publication might be interested in his story for possible post-war publication, but I did not represent any of them.

He then wanted to know if I, myself, would be interested in buying his story—for American dollars.

"I use only rubles in Russia," I answered.

I was curious about what he could do with American dollars. American dollars, he explained, could help him get across the border into Romania, Poland or Finland—Romania and Poland were not yet Iron Curtain countries. He said he had learned this from underground sources.

Stressing that he sorely needed my assistance in carrying out his plans, Mr. K then told me that he wanted to contact a foreign embassy. Understandably, he was afraid to enter any embassy on foot because of the Police and MVD agents who constantly guarded the entrances and closely scrutinized any pedestrian entering the premises. He asked if I would drive him in one evening.

"But how will you get out?" I inquired.

"Oh, they will drive me out, that is, the Embassy people," he answered.

Not wanting to become involved in such a risky escapade, and being a person of high visibility, I gave Mr. K the name, address and telephone number of an adventurous friend of mine who might agree to drive him into the Embassy yard.

Four weeks passed before I saw Mr. K again. Our meeting was arranged by telephone—we had arranged to use oblique hints—and when I met him I asked, "Where have you been all this time?"

"Well, I stayed in the Embassy basement a week. They fed me and interviewed me many times and gave me some clothes. Then I made my way down to the Romanian border. But I couldn't establish any contacts to make it across so I decided to come back to Moscow. It's rather dangerous for a stranger to linger in the border zone. I'm going to try the Finnish border next time."

Four weeks later Mr. K rang me again, so evidently, he had failed to make it across the Finnish frontier. We met on the Leningrad Claussee in Northern Moscow. Mr. K seemed much better dressed, and obviously in foreign clothes. Much of the pallor had left his face and he seemed less uneasy. His air of confidence caused me to wonder if, after all, he really was a fugitive from Kolyma trying to evade the Secret Police.

His story about the Finnish border was the same as what had happened to him in Romania—failure to make the necessary contacts with the proper people. His next attempt, he informed me, would be at the Polish border.

"Good luck," I said, as we parted.

Mr. K never telephoned me again. I do not know whether he succeeded in his attempt to cross the Polish border or whether Secret Police agents captured him and shipped him back to Kolyma.

I have related these meetings exactly as they happened. He told a plausible story. His description of his trials and tribulations was straightforward and consistent. But one question never left my mind during my contacts with the man from Kolyma. Was I flirting with a genuine refugee from a slave labor camp or was I hobnobbing with a master-agent provocateur of the wily Secret Police?

I mentioned these escapades to only one other person, Rembert James, an *Associated Press* man who has been assigned temporarily to the Associated Press Bureau. "You certainly have got something resembling a scoop there," Rembert said. "But watch the cards and play your hand carefully." As an old Russian hand, I hardly needed that advice.

CHAPTER XXII

Odessa Interlude

Where are the girls, mates?
—White U. S. sailor to Negro sailors.

THE WAR IN RUSSIA was perhaps the most mobile in the history of warfare. Great armies of millions of men clashed, recoiled and maneuvered over vast areas in an attempt to destroy or be destroyed. I moved here and there along the long battlefront which stretched for one thousand miles from Leningrad, at the Gulf of Finland, to the Crimea on the Black Sea.

In April, 1944, I found myself in Odessa, Russia's largest seaport on the Black Sea. The Red Army had just liberated the city from the Germans and Romanians. Simultaneously, other Red Army units were storming westwards through Poland, liberating in their path pockets of imprisoned Allied soldiers.

Finding it impossible to repatriate these freed soldiers by land, the Russian authorities had agreed to permit Western transport vessels to pick them up at Odessa. The Western Allies, at the same time, were liberating Russian civilians who had been shipped out of Russia by the Germans

as slave labor for Germany and Occupied Western Europe.
These civilians were now being returned to Odessa. The Allied ships bringing these liberated Russians home were to
take aboard Allied soldiers who had been freed by the Russians.

The transports bringing the Russians through the Mediterranean, the Dardanelles and the Black Sea were escorted by
United States warships. The American sailors were given shore
leave in Odessa, and in the afternoon of the day of the arrival of the first convoy, I found five Negro sailors lounging
in the lobby of the Londres Hotel, where I was staying. One
of them said a white correspondent down at the dock had told
them that I was in town.

I invited them to come up to my room. One of the sailors
produced a deck of cards and I produced two bottles of vodka.
They told me about the war at sea; I filled them in on the war
on the German-Russian front.

Shortly, there came a sharp rapping on the door. Upon my
opening it, three white American seamen from the same ship
as the Negro sailors barged into the room. They appeared to
have had their vodka elsewhere.

"Where are the girls, mates?" one of the white sailors demanded of the Negro sailors.

"I'm sorry, fellows, but there are no girls here," I said.

"Come on, now, don't try to hand us that stuff," one of the
intruders snapped.

One of the white sailors began to explore the bathroom, another peered under the bed and a third threw open the door
of the closet.

We Negroes watched in amused silence. When the white
sailors had finished their unsuccessful search, the oldest of the
Negro sailors, who had a rank, rose up in full stature and said
in a firm voice:

"Now, look here mates. This man is a war correspondent.
He has just told you he is not in the girl business. If you want

to join us, sit down. If you don't, I'll give you just five minutes to clear out of here."

In less than the allotted time, the girl hunters had gone, and we returned to our cards, vodka and interrupted reminiscences.

A few blocks from my hotel, next day I was to stumble onto one of the most touching human dramas of my visit to liberated Odessa. Two armed sentries were standing at the entrance to a school building and, with the usual curiosity of all newsmen, I wanted to find out why a school should need an armed guard.

The sentries offered no objections when I approached the door. And they said or did nothing to prevent my entering the building. My assumption is that they had been informed that Allied war correspondents were in the city and that they were not to be interfered with. Or maybe it was because I was a Negro.

I walked down one of the corridors and hearing talk through the open door of one of the classrooms, I entered. To my surprise, there were several couples in the room—Australians and New Zealanders, one Britisher—and Russian women.

After introducing myself, the men told me they had been captured by the Germans during the ill-fated Greek campaign early in the war and had been held prisoners in Poland and East Prussia ever since. The Red Army, in its westward drive, had freed them and sent them overland to Odessa to board one of the Allied repatriation ships.

The Russian women, who were actually their wives, had been shipped out of Russia by the Germans as slave laborers in 1941. They had met their husbands while working at forced labor in Poland and East Prussia and married them there. Their marriage certificates, which they showed me, were signed by Polish Catholic priests, testifying that all had been legally joined in wedlock.

Speaking Russian fluently, I was able to talk directly with

the wives. They told me they were all from South Russia and had been captured over an area extending from Odessa to Rostov-on-Don. Their ages ranged from twenty to twenty-five.

"Don't you find life cooped up in this school building rather inconvenient?" I asked.

"Ochen! (very)," three of them answered in unison.

Then I made an almost unbelievable discovery.

Why don't you go out into the city?" I asked.

"*Nerazreshaetsa* (not permitted)!" two answered simultaneously.

Wishing to confirm this, I turned to the other women.

"Sovershenno verno (it's quite true)," two of them affirmed.

"Is it your husbands who won't allow you to go out into the city?"

"Nyet! Nyet!" one of the women answered. "It's the guards."

Then I asked the husbands if this was true.

"That's quite right, old bloke. They are telling you the truth," one Australian said.

"Do you mean to say you haven't been outside this building since you arrived here one week ago?"

"Once they let us go to the market a few blocks down the street to buy some fruit and vegetables, but we had an armed escort."

I knew that the repatriation ship was scheduled to sail the next day, so I remarked, "Well, young ladies, you'll soon be out on the big sea on the way to your new homes. Aren't you happy?"

Their reaction was complete and gloomy silence.

"Brother," interposed an Australian, "I've learned a little Russian from my wife and I understood what you just said. Sit here a little longer and let me tell you something interesting."

As we sat on the edge of a bed by the window he told me the following poignant story.

Briefly, it was this. They were all in love with their wives and their wives were in love with them. They had worked and suffered together in Nazi captivity. Some of the soldiers had arrived wounded at their place of imprisonment and the Russian women had nursed them back to health. The men were allies of Russia. Yet every effort was being made by the Russian authorities to prevent the women from going aboard ship with their husbands.

"What do you intend doing about it?" I asked.

"One thing is certain," he answered. "We have all decided that we are not going to board any ship unless our wives can go with us."

The war was moving westward and I had to move with it. I could not tarry to learn the final outcome of the manful stand taken by these Allied soldiers to prevent disruption of their marriages by the Russian authorities. But I have often wondered how they made out.

CHAPTER XXIII

Maidenek:
Rendezvous with Death

Abandon all hope ye who enter here.
—Dante's *Divine Comedy*

ALL DURING THE WAR I had heard reports that the German Nazis were spreading death among the civilian populations of European countries. I had heard of a chain of extermination camps—Buchenwald, Belsen, Auschwitz, etc.—in which millions of human beings were annihilated in assembly line fashion.

I wondered: Was this wartime propaganda? Was it actually happening? All doubt was soon removed by my visit to one of these ghastly extermination camps—Maidanek, in southeastern Poland. "Mission Macabre" is what I called this assignment.

The dependable American lend-lease DC–47 workhorse, with large red stars of the Soviet Air Force painted on its sides and wings, was churning its way westwards from Moscow in the summer of 1944. The plane had no defenses of its own, so the hard-pressed Russians had managed to spare two of their excellent YAK fighter planes as a protective escort.

The need for this escort was understandable—we were flying westwards into Poland, where the Red Army was pressing on Warsaw. What a prize it would have been for the Germans to force down and capture a large segment of Western Allied war correspondents who had been reporting the war from Russia!

All of a sudden the plane began a rapid descent, and as I looked out I could see the YAK escorts peeling away. The plane was over a great forest near the Russian-Polish border, which made it impossible for the pilot to follow his instructions to make a quick landing in case of danger. In case a landing was impossible, his orders were to continue flying at just above tree-top level. As I looked down on the nearby tree tops, I realized something untoward had happened, but did not know what.

About an hour later, a landing was made on a hot and dusty airstrip near Lublin, Poland, southeast of Warsaw. I asked one of the Russian crewmen what had happened. He told me that two German fighter planes had been reported flying in our direction and that our YAK escort had peeled off to do battle with the Germans and thus draw them away from our plane. The two YAKS arrived at the airstrip a short time afterwards, and I presumed they had won the battle with the Germans or at least had driven them off.

Jeeps soon had us in Lublin, ancient Polish city and seat of an old and famous Catholic university. I was housed in a room with John Fisher, an Australian who was writing for a London newspaper, in a two-story building just off the campus of the university.

Not far from this was another well-fenced-in building that a Pole suggested I visit. It had been, he said, some kind of secret German bureau and was now abandoned. I descended into the basement and found the corridors lined with barred cells, all now unlocked. On the walls of several I saw messages, in Polish, which I could not understand. They appeared to be written in blood. This must have been a Gestapo prison.

One of the most striking things I noticed about Lublin was that though the Germans had occupied and ruled this part of Poland since 1939, the Poles seemed better dressed and better fed than the civilians in Russia. The peasant markets were well-stocked with all kinds of farm produce. The men wore fairly good clothes and many of the Polish women could be said to be smartly dressed.

The favorable food situation can be explained by the fact that Poland had not had any collective farms and the Germans not only permitted but encouraged private farming. The Germans, I recalled, had planned to disband the collective farms in the occupied Soviet Ukraine and this had gained them much cooperation from the individualistic and nationalistic Ukrainian peasants.

My schedule for the next day was to visit Maidanek, a short drive outside Lublin. The trip was made in an American Dodge, a four-wheel drive lend-lease military vehicle driven by a Polish chauffeur, with a lovely blond Polish Jewish girl of about nineteen sitting alongside me. She spoke both English and German and was to act as interpreter. Her name was Rachel Summerstein.

"How did you escape being harmed by the Germans?" I asked her. I would have considered it rather unfeeling to have said murdered.

"I managed to hide out in different sections of the forest and in several other places near Cracow. Some Poles helped to hide me and my father, too. Look!" she exclaimed, pointing. "There is Maidanek. Some of my relatives and friends . . ." She gulped and could not finish the sentence.

In the distance I saw low, green, barrack-like buildings, much like one might find at any army camp. As a matter of fact, there were one hundred and forty-four of these buildings, each with a housing capacity of three hundred persons. The most conspicious thing was a large square, red-brick chimney that I judged to be about two hundred feet high. As

we approached, I saw that the whole area was enclosed with
double rows of barbed-wire ten feet tall. I later learned
that the wire had been electrified when the Germans were
there.

Spaced out along the fence were twenty-foot-high watch-
towers, each with a powerful searchlight. I later learned that
in case any inmates managed to escape, two hundred savage
German police dogs were ready to take up the chase.

We passed slowly through a wide open gate into the com-
pound. A deathly stillness seemed to brood over the place. I
was inside one of Nazi Germany's most notorious though little
known extermination camps—where an estimated 1,500,000
human beings from all over Europe had expired. A large proportion of the victims had been Jews. The German name for
the camp was "Vernichtungslager" (Extermination Camp).

A German named Hans was to be my guide. He spoke understandable English. It appeared that Hans had not been on
good terms with his Nazi officers—perhaps he had tried to
show signs of humanity towards the inmates—and when the
Germans retreated from Maidanek he was either left behind
or decided to remain. Hans claimed that he had been forced
to work at Maidanek and that he had found the work highly
disagreeable.

"But I had to obey orders," Hans kept repeating. "If I hadn't
well, . . ." he pointed to his breast with his hand in imita-
tion of a pistol.

First, I was given a general orientation tour of the camp.
The details were to come later—and what sadistic details they
were. I took a casual look through the registration building just
inside the gate, the bathhouse nearby, the barracks with their
tiers of bunks, and finally circled the furnace and its tall brick
chimney.

The Germans have always prided themselves on being a very
efficient and methodical people; they had built and organized
this camp in ways that would have delighted a management

and efficiency expert. They had even set up a small "museum" for cataloguing and exhibiting the documents taken off the condemned.

After returning to my starting point, I had a feeling that I had seen enough. Yet, I had made only a cursory survey; my assignment would have been incomplete without my taking notebook and pencil and following the death route—from living human beings to human ashes. I asked to go into the "museum" first.

Here were tens of thousands of identification cards, most of them with small photographs attached. A wide range of ages was represented; the youngest victim that I noted had been fourteen, the oldest had been eighty. The faces of young men and women in the flower of youth looked up at me, seemingly pensively from glass-covered cases.

Almost every country in Europe then occupied by the Germans was represented—Greece, Holland, France, Yugoslavia, Denmark, Norway, Belgium, Poland and the Baltic States. There were also victims from amongst Germany's allies—no doubt they had been opposed to Nazi Germany and the collaborating regimes that Germany supported in such countries. Many of the names indicated that the victims had been Jewish —not only from Poland, but also from each of the above named countries.

Suddenly, I was startled for before me were army identifications with pictures of black men in the uniform of the French army! République Française! I enquired of Hans how these black men had happened to reach distant Maidanek. His explanation was plausible and convincing.

The French army had always had a strong Senegalese segment—tall, brave and dependable soldiers. They had been deployed in defense of France's Maginot Line Fortifications in northeastern France at the beginning of the war. This great defense works, with its massive turrets, powerful guns and network of interconnected underground ramifications, had been considered impregnable, able to withstand any assault indefinitely.

But when Hitler made his blitzkreig invasion of France in 1940, his armies outflanked the Maginot Line, trapping many of the Senegalese troops in the process. Being the extreme racist that he was, Hitler must have decided that these black men must be destroyed utterly and without trace.

All that remained of them now were their army tickets and their photographs; their ashes had fallen through the grates of the huge furnace at Maidanek. I was unable to find out how many Senegalese had been cremated or when, but they must have been exterminated in 1942 when the first two furnaces began operating. I believe that I was the first, if not the only, correspondent to report the ultimate fate of these Senegalese soldiers.

When victims arrived at Maidanek they were told, after registration, that they must take a routine bath for delousing. I walked across the narrow camp street to take a look at one of the six large oblong bath halls. Two of the halls were adaptable for the use of carbon monoxide. When all the halls were operating at full capacity, they could kill one hundred and ninety persons at one time. Looking up, I noticed rows of perforated pipes overhead. No person who ever entered one of these halls to take a "bath" came out alive.

In the doors at each end of the halls were square "peep windows" through which the Germans watched the "bathing" —and its effect.

After the bathers lined up under the overhead water pipes and the warm water began showering down, a crystalline powder called "Zyklon" (which I took to be German for cyclone) began sifting down from holes in the ceiling. When it dissolved in the steam, it created a poisonous blue mist that had the same effect on the wet, warm bodies as hydrocyanic acid. Death came quickly and silently.

Afterwards the bodies were loaded onto a trailer, crosswise

onto

oor
ed
a

...ractor pulled them away to the roaring

...was told, were cremated without first going
...s because they refused to undress in front of
...s of the Nazi guards. "To the furnace!" a Ger-
...would order, and the unfortunate women were
...ay screaming.

...d through the bathhouse and followed the route of
...ler to the furnace, about a half mile away.

...hen I asked Hans the reason for the baths, since the vic-
...s were doomed to death in the furnace anyway, he an-
...vered, "It was considered more humane. Besides, to herd the
people alive directly to the furnace would have meant screams
and commotion. Also the gold had to be extracted from their
teeth, their hair cut off and their clothes carefully gone over.
And those in charge wanted to keep this operation as quiet as
possible. They didn't want any screams to be heard outside."
However, occasionally there were screams from the barracks,
in which case the Germans turned on loud jazz music through
loudspeakers.

In other words, the true nature of Maidanek was to be
kept a secret, with not even Poles living in the neighborhood
knowing exactly what was transpiring there. Thus it had
been arranged that convoys of prisoners arrived only after
dark.

The crematorium was built of red bricks and was about
fifteen feet high. It had only two incinerators at first; five more
were added in 1943. The consuming fire, with the aid of an
electric blower fan, could be stepped up to 1500 degrees of
heat Centigrade. Across from the furnace doors, on a cemented
and walled patio, stood several wheeled stretchers.

It was here that gold teeth were yanked out of victim's
mouths and women's hair cut off. After this, the bodies were
rolled on the stretchers to the furnace doors, which were about
two feet above the floor. The stretchers fitted flush with the

bottom of the furnace doors, making it easy to slide bodies
the furnace gratings.

I was told that four bodies could be fed through each o
at the same time, thereby speeding up the work. It requi
fifteen minutes to incinerate four bodies. The furnace had
rated capacity, when working at full speed, of reducing 2,00
bodies to ashes daily. Coal was used as fuel.

I passed around to the back side of the furnace, looked down
into the pits and still there were the gray ashes—no doubt of
the last victims to be exterminated before the Red Army captured the camp.

A short distance behind the furnace was a large vegetable
garden. I walked through it and never before had I seen such
huge tomatoes, cabbages, turnips, onion, radishes and other
vegetables. When I asked Hans why, he answered, "Human
ashes make the finest fertilizer in the world."

Then I wanted to know what was done with this large supply of vegetables.

"Well, the German guards billeted at the camp ate most of
them and the surplus was fed to prisoners. Not all the arriving
prisoners could be put directly through the bathhouse and furnace. They often created a backlog that had to be housed in
those barracks over there to wait their turn. They had to be
fed."

A short distance away I noticed what looked like a pile of
slag. I moved over and found thousands of pairs of shoes of all
sizes, shapes and styles—women's, children's slippers, men's
shoes and high upper shoes for both sexes. All of them showed
signs of wear. I was later to learn what happened to shoes in
good condition.

Near the fence were a few yawning pits with some bones
still sticking out of the earth. The Nazis had been commiting
executions in this camp even before the furnace was put into
operation. And even after it began operating, if the backlog
became too great to be accommodated by the furnace, hundreds

of prisoners were shot or asphyxiated by carbon monoxide gas and buried in common graves.

It was a great relief to leave the Maidanek extermination camp and return to my quarters in Lublin.

The next day I was to find out what happened to good footwear. I was taken by Rachel to a large warehouse on Chopin Street near the center of Lublin. I found it full of shelves, reaching to the ceiling, and large tables on which were piled all kinds of shoes, women's, men's and children's clothes, jewelry, human hair, watches, bracelets, broaches, gold rings, underwear, socks and women's stockings and a mass of other personal effects. The labels on some of the goods revealed that they had come from shops in Vienna, Athens, Paris, Antwerp, Amsterdam, Warsaw, Kiev and other European cities.

Lists were distributed to German families in Germany, with descriptions and sizes of these goods and their prices. German buyers simply filled in an order blank, sent the money and the goods were packed and shipped to them mail-order fashion to a delivery station at Plötzensee-Berlin, Strafanstalt. It was as simple as that; though it was most certainly a grisly morally-tainted business.

I was notified that next day the Polish-born, Red Army Marshal K. K. Rokossovsky would review units of the new Polish Army on Lublin's main street. I took up a vantage point almost directly across the street from the reviewing stand, along with another American and a Chinese correspondent.

As the Polish troops marched past, with Marshal Rokossovsky taking the salute from a raised platform, my companions and I began making descriptive notes in our notebooks. A Russian MP immediately came up and demanded that we give them to him. We categorically refused. He continued to insist.

The incident attracted the attention of several Poles who were standing nearby, and they came to our defense. Now, Poles have never had any love for Russians. Furthermore, they found it disagreeable seeing armed Russians patrolling the streets of their ancient city. Older Poles spoke fairly understandable Russian, making it possible for me to understand them.

"What's going on here?" one of them asked in Russian.

I explained, in Russian, as the Poles encircled us, as if to protect us. One of them lashed out verbally at the overly-suspicious Russian MP.

"Don't you know who these men are, Russky?" he asked, pointing at us. The Russian remained silent.

"Are you so dumb you don't know who is in town?" he continued, with the Russian still pointing his gun in our direction.

The other Poles were greatly agitated, too, and were heatedly berating the Russian in Polish.

"Well, if you don't know, I'll tell you," the Russian-speaking Pole shouted. "These men are Allied journalists. They are our guests. Now you get away from here with that damned gun and don't bother them anymore."

The Russian MP saluted, stepped back, saluted again, wheeled around and marched briskly off down the sidewalk, with the Poles guffawing at his unwarranted show of authority.

Before my departure from Lublin, Rachel introduced me to her father, Samuel Summerstein. He was a weather-beaten, middle-aged Jew who before the war had been active in Polish Jewish life. He was deeply concerned over what had happened to Jews in Russia. He knew what had happened to Jews in Germany and Poland. He also inquired about Jews in America. I gave him all the information I possessed, including the slaughter of the Jews in Kiev when the Germans captured that Ukrainian city, with its large Jewish population.

"Please write to me after you get back to Moscow," were Rachel's parting words before my Jeep left for the airstrip to board the DC–47 that was to fly me back to Moscow.

I have heard that some of the Germans responsible for the

mass exterminations at Maidanek were captured and turned over to Polish authorities after the war. They were executed; they deserved it. I also understand that the Poles did not raze the Maidanek extermination camp—they decided to keep it almost exactly as the Germans left it, as a stark reminder of Nazi Germany's Herringvolk savagery.

CHAPTER XXIV

Paul Robeson's Brother-in-law

A sadder and wiser man. . . .
—Coleridge

ON A BITTER-COLD January evening in 1945, as I sat working on some of my wartime notes, the doorbell of my Moscow apartment rang. It was not my practice to answer my bell because beggars, some of them Red Army soldiers demobilized from wounds or on leave, had been very annoying to the tenants in the building. Some of these soldiers were outright beggars; others offered for sale wrist watches, jewelry and other small "trophies" they had looted from East European countries that the Red Army had overrun.

But the ringing persisted, so I decided to take a look. In the doorway loomed a huge figure in a coarse black cotton padded overcoat, black fur cap with the earflaps dangling loose and wearing valenkis, the knee-high felt Russian boots. In the dim light of the staircase the massive figure made me think of a big grizzly bear.

The caller turned out to be Paul Robeson's brother-in-law, whom I had not seen since before the war. Frank Goode had come to Russia in 1936 on a visit to the country where Paul

Robeson was a regular, highly-honored and much ballyhooed visitor.

Goode was a great hulk of a man, more than six feet tall, with broad and powerful shoulders, long arms and ham-like hands. He must have weighed more than two hundred pounds. A scowling expression covered his bronze face and this was accentuated by his hair which came down to a Mephistophelian point on his forehead. I always felt that Goode could have made a fortune had he been properly trained and gone into heavyweight boxing in America.

One day, shortly after his arrival in Moscow, a sharp-eyed scout for the Moscow Circus caught sight of Goode and knowing an unmistakable attraction when he saw one, made him an attractive offer to join a string of husky Russian wrestlers then touring the country.

Goode knew nothing about wrestling, but the circus scout felt that despite this Goode would prove a great box-office attraction. His guess proved correct, for packed houses turned out in every city where Goode appeared with the Russian matmen. Huge posters went up announcing the early arrival of the black Ajax, or Hercules, or Samson—with a picture of Goode in a muscular stance.

In every city the troupe visited the referee called for volunteers from among the spectators to come forward and test their muscular powers against Goode. Sometimes there were volunteers, but with more bravado than determination. They'd start toward the ring, lose their nerve and hurriedly return to their seats. A brawny Cossack miner in the Donbas coal-mining district actually reached the ring and was beginning to climb through the ropes. But when he looked up and saw the huge towering bulk of the so-called "Black Samson" peering down at him, with arms and legs akimbo, he lost heart and literally ran back to his seat, with the jeers of "trus" (coward) filling the arena.

The wrestling troupe traveled all over Russia with tremen-

dous success. Goode had plenty of loose money, and a way with
buxom Russian women. He later married a woman with whom
he became acquainted in Batum, near the Turkish border. She
was an oriental type, and Goode told me her eyes had trans-
fixed and hypnotized him. I believe that his wife actually was
Turkish.

He brought her to Moscow and set her up in style. But
those "transfixing and hypnotizing eyes," it seems, began to
work their magic in other directions. The match did not last
long—Goode said he had good grounds for suspecting that she
was making love with another man and they later parted.

Goode liked Russia so much that he told me he never intended leaving the country. His mat work supplied him with
great wads of rubles and he stayed in the best hotels. He was
one of the country's best-dressed men for he received from London regular supplies of the best quality British clothes and
shoes from his brother-in-law, Paul Robeson, and his sister,
Mrs. Eslanda Goode Robeson. "Man, this is the life for me,"
he once remarked to me.

Then came the war. Goode's wrestling troupe was disbanded and the wrestlers were left to shuffle for themselves.
Joe Stalin was now engaged in a mortal wrestling match with
his old ally, Adolf Hitler and there was no time or money now
to be devoted to any other wrestling activities.

It was a hungry and cold and depressed American Negro
whom I let into my apartment on that bitter-cold January evening in 1945. After he took off his overcoat, I could see that
his former bulk had shrunken to smaller proportions. While he
was warming himself at my radiator, my wife went to the
kitchen to prepare him a meal. I helped him pull off his valenkis and instead of wearing socks, his feet were wrapped in
pieces of rags.

He quickly disposed of everything on the table, including
caviar washed down with deep gulps of vodka. He now got
around to telling me of his wartime tribulations.

With nothing to do in western Russia after the war started, he and two of his husky wrestling partners decided to evacuate to the area east of the Ural Mountains. In the cities there he had to sell his good British clothes and shoes in order to buy food (he had always had a Gargantuan appetite) and soon he was loaded with large sums of rubles. The Russians believed that Stalin had fled the Kremlin and was in a hideout somewhere far away from the roar of guns and that the Germans would soon be masters of the country. Believing this, and expecting that the ruble would thereby soon become worthless, they began freely unloading rubles for anything of value.

But fate played an expensive trick on Goode. Although he was receiving large sums for his good clothes and shoes in the cities, he later found that Russian peasants would not accept rubles for their eggs, butter, milk, chickens, bread and other foodstuffs. The peasant economy had gone over almost wholly to barter, and soap, tea, sugar, flour, coffee, jewelry and articles of clothing had become the favored trading media.

Goode now had none of these things. He and his wrestling partners, both of whom had had some experience as cobblers, turned to making light summer sandals and winter valenkis out of any scrap material they could forage. These they then bartered for food.

They also later did some heavy wrestling with inanimate objects—unloading freight cars of Lend-Lease supplies that were reaching Russia through Vladivostok. This back-breaking work earned them rubles, some of which they spent for items of food, whenever these could be found. The rest of their rubles they stashed away for the time, if the war were not lost, when the ruble would return to its former value.

With the war now moving across eastern Europe into Germany, Goode decided to come back to Moscow. There has always been a belief in Russia that though food may be scarce elsewhere in the country, at least black bread and a few other items could always be found in Moscow if one hunted long enough. There was much truth in that belief, for I recall that during the famine years of the thirties, black bread and some other foodstuffs could always be found somewhere in the city.

Arriving back in Moscow, Goode made straight for my house. He was lucky to find me in, for I had just returned two days before from one of the battle zones. He had known that I, as a foreign correspondent having access to the special Diplomatic Food Shop, where food and drink were always in plentiful supply, would have a full cupboard. He also knew that he could give me rubles to buy him a few bottles of vodka (which was very scarce in the city) in that same shop. With this Russian firewater he could make some profitable barter deals, for vodka had a higher purchasing power than money.

After clearing my table, Goode reclined on my divan with a heavy stomach and a pensive mind. I told him he could spend the night there if he wished, but he declined, saying he had a place downtown to bunk with an old circus friend.

"Well, Frank, it now looks as if the war will soon be over," I said. "What are your after-war plans?"

"Brother, I wouldn't mind going home," he replied. "But I now have a Soviet passport; do you think they would let me leave? Remember, I used to wear fine Scotch woolen suits and the best English shoes? But just look at me now—dressed like most Russians, worse than some. It never crossed my mind before the war that I would ever come to this."

It was getting late now, and Goode began wrapping the rags around his feet before pulling on his valenkis. I opened a chest draw and threw him a pair of heavy woolen socks. Out of my wardrobe I took a pair of oversize GI shoes and a GI winter shirt, both of which were too large for me. I also handed him a pair of fur-lined leather mittens, but he couldn't get his ham-like hands into them. I told him to take them along anyway and trade them at a peasant market for food.

My wife prepared a few sandwiches from some canned cheese and ham. A spare bottle of vodka was found. But I never saw Frank Goode again before I left Russia after the end of the war. I understand he returned to wrestling for awhile and again began wearing quality clothes and shoes sent him by Paul Robeson and his sister Eslanda. My last report was that he now lives in Gorky, not far from Moscow, with his second wife and teen-aged daughter, subsisting mainly on the government pension earned during his years as a wrestler.

Another American Negro that had been in Russia when I got there was Robert (Bob) Ross. It was generally assumed that he had been brought over by the American Communist Party and the International Labor Defense Organization, because during the Scottsboro trouble he toured Russia making speeches in defense of the boys. He maintained close relations with influential Communists and Communist Youth Organizations and from all reports never suffered any change of heart or mind about his adopted country. He had two daughters by his first wife and when I left Russia he was living with his second wife.

CHAPTER XXV

Out the Window

We are less convinced by what we hear than by what we see.
—Herodotus

WHEN THE WAR ENDED victoriously for Russia and her Western Allies, I found myself faced with a decision. Should I remain in Russia? Or should I leave and go to the job that was waiting for me in Ethiopia? The Ethiopian Minister in Moscow, Blattengueta Lorenz Taezaz, my very close friend, had told me that an Ethiopian visa would be issued whenever I wanted it.

Any desire of remaining was predicated upon the hope that the regime might not return to its pre-war civilian repressions. If ever a people had deserved and earned the right to democratic freedoms, it was the Russian people. They had suffered terribly during the war. They had endured hunger and had toiled desperately for victory in what they had been told was a "patriotic war in defense of the Russian motherland." Casualties had been in the neighborhood of twenty million, with seven and a half million killed.

At one time I had entertained the idea that if the Kremlin showed any indication of turning Russia into a really democratic country, I would not mind remaining. But I was soon to be disappointed. Hardly had the war ended before the old repressions began re-appearing. And this recalled my once having heard old Bolshevik Maxim Litvinov remark that "We Marxists have our own ideas about democracy and freedom."

The Secret Police resumed their old ruthlessness. Stalin warned the people not to let their heads "go into a whirl" over victory or be influenced by their war-time contacts with Western countries. He made it clear that the only task ahead now was to resume the building of Communism—with all that implied in further sacrifices and hardships.

The regime had ways of giving advance hints of what could be expected. For example, only a few months after the end of the war, the Central Committee of the Communist Party adopted and published a resolution warning Soviet literary publications and Soviet writers against admiring and kowtowing to the "poisoned, decadent, rotten and narrow and petty literature of the West."

The leading literary monthly, *Zvezda* (Star), was "reformed"; the literary monthly, *Leningrad*, was simply liquidated. And two of Russia's leading writers, Anna Akhmatova and Michael Zoschenko, both contributors to these two publications, were singled out as scapegoats and accused of having become enamored of and contaminated by "bourgeois ideology." They were toppled from their literary pinnacle and consigned to the literary wilderness.

There was no mistaking what these emerging repressions presaged. Russians had become habituated, through long years of experience, to reading between the lines; to them these incidents forewarned that the blissful days of admiration for and collaboration with foreign Allies had terminated. And from that time on, the anti-foreign campaign—later to become the cold war—soon reached the proportions of a crusade.

Another repressive and forewarning measure—though it was not officially admitted at the time—was the rounding up and shipping en masse from the Crimea to Siberia of the entire Tartar population—men, women and children. When an official admission of this deportation was made later, it was alleged that the Tartars had collaborated with the Germans and Romanians during their occupancy of the Crimea.

The Crimean Tartars, among whom I had made friends during my vacations in the Crimea, had lived there since the Golden Horde had invated Russia back in the 14th century. When these Mongol invaders were making their final retreat eastward from Central Russia, one wing retreated to the south and settled in the Crimean Peninsula. But these deep roots in the Crimea did not save them from Stalin's wrath.

The Russian people, I found, always had a deep admiration for America and everything American. Some of my Russian friends used to say, "I would like to see America—then die." And I shall never forget the remark made to me by a Russian woman one night during a blackout near the end of the war. I felt that she was talking for all the Russian people.

She and I were waiting at a bus stop on Gorky Street, across from the Central Telegraph Office. The bus was a long time in coming, and we began complaining to each other about the delay. Hearing my foreign accent, she asked where I came from. I told her I was an American war correspondent. Priyartno" (it's pleasant), she responded. Coming closer—as if she feared somebody might be nearby in the dark—she spoke in an undertone.

"When you go back to America, please tell President Roosevelt and the American people that ordinary Russians thank them from the very bottom of our hearts, for what they have done for us. If it had not been for their help, millions of us would have starved to death. Without the American military help, Hitler might have won the war against our country. But there are certain people who will forget all this as soon as victory is in their pockets."

What the extent of that American help was, the ordinary

Russian people had not forgotten—though it was never widely publicized in Russia. The United States supplied Russia during the war with 14,700 planes, 7,000 tanks, 375,000 trucks, 186 naval vessels, 52,000 Jeeps and 35,000 motorcycles. Mountains of foodstuffs were sent from America, much of which did indeed save large numbers of Russians from starvation.

When news of the death of President Roosevelt reached Russia, I saw more tears shed by ordinary Russians than had been shed since the death of Lenin in 1924. Russians can become very emotional, and some of my Russian friends actually cried on my shoulders.

When I arrived in Russia, I recall, there definitely was more egalitarianism existing among the people. I remember that Red Army officers used to wear identical uniforms and boots as privates. There was no saluting of officers.

Full and admirable camaraderie prevailed in all spheres of civilian life, though, of course, the former bourgeoisie were treated as second-class citizens. While it was true that many hardships and privations were widespread, these were shared more or less equally and this made them all the more bearable. Little or no class distinctions were observed.

Reports coming out of Russia today indicate that the class of the intelligentsia—scientists, professors, engineers, writers, doctors, leading theatrical people and technicians—has become influential and class-conscious, with its own vested interests. By the time of Stalin's death in 1953, a majority, about seventy per cent, of the deputies in the Supreme Soviet (Parliament) were from the intelligentsia. High-ranking military men, if not a class, appear to have become a caste. Then, of course, there always has been the ruling class—the Communist Party. The present class stratifications would seem to leave the workers and peasants at the bottom.

Friction between the majority Russians and the many different minority racial groups was conspicuously absent. Anti-

Semitism, long deep-rooted in Russia, appeared to have had its ugly head chopped off. "Tovarisch" (Comrade) was the favorite and ordinary form of address everywhere. (The word "Tovarisch" was an anathema to the former aristocracy who, at least among themselves, used as a salutation "Gospodin" (Mister) or "Grazhdanin" (Citizen).

The few American Negroes living and working in Russia were great favorites with the Russian people. These Negroes, like many other Americans, wanted to be loved and the Russians gave them in full measure the love they felt they had been denied them in the United States.

Unlike many of the white Americans, who spent much of their time bumping into one another in the downtown hotels, Negroes spent their leisure time out among the Russian toiling masses. And this inevitably accounted for the noticeable fact that Negroes learned the difficult Russian language quicker and spoke it far more fluently than their white compatriots.

Negroes were coddled everywhere (it was sincere) and appeared to have been presented the keys to the city. They seemed, understandably, to revel in using these keys with gusto and satisfaction, sometimes—also understandably—without proper savoir-faire. They had no fear that anybody would tread on their toes. But by and large, Negroes were disciplined and industrious in carrying out their contractual tasks, and this the Russians greatly admired. It was to them an example of how Americans got things done.

Despite the fact that there were fewer of the material amenities in Russia than they had known in America, I never heard any of these Negroes make any complaints about life in Russia. There were shortages of everything; there was none of the freedom of speech they had known in the United States. Yet, Negroes felt that the full racial equality they were experiencing fully compensated for any material shortcomings.

They genuinely liked Russia and the Russian people. But when Stalin began his great purges in the late 1930's and foreign technicians began to leave Russia, most Negroes began patting their American passports and studying train and boat schedules. Today, as far as I have been able to ascertain, only five hard-core American Negro expatriates remain in Russia.

I, too, had become very fond of and well-disposed toward Russia and the likeable Russian people. It could hardly have been otherwise; non-discrimination and non-segregation could not possibly generate anything other than satisfaction, good will and gratefulness. The harshness of the regime, of course, could not be overlooked; but this did not affect me or other Negroes directly.

Perusing some of my dispatches of those Russian years, I have found that most of them were written in a spirit of good will. What I liked and considered praiseworthy, I lauded. I was honest and most likely, under similar circumstances, I would have written in the same vein had the Czar still been Russia's ruler.

I was not alone in this respect. Most of the distinguished correspondents for large American newspapers in Moscow— Walter Duranty, Eugene Lyons, Louis Fischer, and others— also wrote favorably about the "new experiment" in Russia. And what they wrote was being published.

Of course, it was common knowledge, to Russians and foreigners alike, that Stalin's Secret Police were regularly making nocturnal calls. Hundreds of thousands of Russians were being shipped to the vast network of concentration camps in Siberia and in other "distant places," as the Russians called such camps. One might ask, then, why did not the foreign correspondents write about this? The answer is simple. Strict censorship, without any prospect of anything critical escaping the censor's sharp eyes.

Over the years, I had witnessed great changes occurring in Russia. A huge heavy-industry base was built—with large contributions in machinery and technical skills from Western Europe and the United States.

When I arrived, Russia ranked low among the industrial countries of the world, unable even to supply her own basic industrial needs for two Five Year Plans. Today, only nineteen years after World War II, Russia is a great industrial power, ranking first in Europe and second in the world. Only the United States exceeds Russia in the production of steel, iron ore, crude petroleum, cement, lead, pig iron, ferrous alloys, and electric power generating capacity. This undeniably is no mean achievement for a country which, before the 1917 Revolution, was considered backward and undeveloped.

One of the great paradoxes of this achievement was that Capitalism was providing enormous amounts of machinery and a large number of engineers and technicians for laying the basis for Russia's industrialization. Without this vital aid, Stalin's Five Year Plans might have failed. And such a failure could have generated internal unrest and possibly even domestic political repercussions.

Ships arriving at Leningrad, Odessa and Vladivostok were loaded to capacity with the finest and most modern capitalist machinery. Foreign engineers and technicians were pouring into Russia from America, Germany, England, France and Italy to lend their knowledge and skills to strengthening the foundations of Communism.

Among these technicians were several Negroes who, because of the lack of opportunity of plying their trade in the United States, had availed themselves of the absence of prejudice in Russia. One of these was Richard Williams, an electrical engineer from New York City, who arrived in Moscow in 1934 to fill a job awaiting him with the Commissariat (Ministry) of Heavy Industry. Just over the Ural Mountains sprawls one of the world's greatest steel works—the Magnitogorsk Metallurgical Works. This vast steel complex was built by American and German engineers and its furnaces, machinery and other heavy equipment were supplied by the United States and Germany. This was the plant where Dick Williams was sent as a maintenance engineer. Robert Robinson, who had been working at the Ford Motor Company in Detroit, was also offered a contract by the Soviet Union as an engineer. As an expert in fine tolerance instruments, he has over twenty-seven industrial inventions to his credit. George Tynes, a skilled agronomist and graduate of Wilberforce University, is technical director of a game reserve. He is now considered the leading Soviet authority on geese, chickens and ducks, but in those days he was just one of a large number of foreign experts pouring into the Soviet Union to contribute their skills and know-how to assist in the industrialization of Stalin's Russia.

In Nizhni-Novgorod, on the Volga, I visited Russia's first automobile plant. I found that it had been designed, built and put into operation by Henry Ford's engineers and technicians. Ford had handed over his patents for use in this enormous plant, which had a rated capacity of producing 100,000 automobiles annually.

This plant was one of the early giants of Stalin's First Five Year Plan, built willingly—at a solid profit, of course—by one of the great tycoons of American capitalism.

Simultaneously, American engineers and technicians, under the leadership of Colonel Hugh L. Cooper, were building the great Dnieper Hydroelectric Power Station on the Dnieper River in the Ukraine. The great project required five years to build and its towering dam was exceeded in size only by the Boulder Dam Hydroelectric installation. When completed the Dnieper Station was the second largest hydroelectric power station in the world.

The General Electric Company supplied the turbines for this giant power station under an agreement signed with the Soviet Government in 1928. For financing the great project, the General Electric Company arranged for advancing to the Soviet Government credits totaling $25,000,000, according to Louis Fischer's *The Soviets In World Affairs*.

After completion of the power station in the early 1930's,

a vast complex of steel, aluminum and chemical plants sprang up near the site, most of their machinery and equipment also provided by Western capitalism.

While I was in Russia the country's two greatest tractor plants—one at Stalingrad, the other at Kharkov—were designed, built and put into operation by American engineers and technicians. Sixty per cent of the machinery at the Kharkov tractor plant came from the United States and besides American, British, German and French engineers assisted in construction of this great plant.

In 1938 I visited the Rostov Agricultural Machinery Plant at Rostov-On-Don. This great plant sprawled over more than four hundred acres and manufactured plows, harvesters, harrows, caterpillar and wheeled tractors and other farm implements. Had it not been for the Russian workers around me, I could have been in an American agricultural machinery plant.

Most of the machinery was American made and the system of conveyors, belts and assembly lines gave the whole place an American atmosphere. Thanks to the foreign designing skill and know-how and the ultra-modern machines in the plant, it served well—and may still be serving—in producing thousands of caterpillar treads for the Red Army's heavy tanks.

When American Ambassador Joseph E. Davies, as he reported in *Mission To Moscow,* visited the plant in the summer of 1938, he was not admitted to one large section, being told that it was not in operation because of repairs in progress. But it was assumed in American circles that this section of the plant, instead of being under repairs, was being switched over to the production of armaments. Nor was it assumed that the large tractor plants at Stalingrad and Kharkov were wholly engaged in making peaceful agricultural machinery.

I have mentioned these few industrial enterprises as but a few typical examples of how Capitalism had rendered yeomen's service to the industrial foundations of Stalin's Russia. There were dozens of other heavy and light industrial plants that I visited—and it was surprising to see on most of them labels reading "Made In U.S.A.," "Made In Germany," "Made In England," etc.

Hundreds, perhaps thousands—the exact figure has never been published—of capitalistic engineers and technicians were engaged in building Russian industry, including oil and mining. And much of this feverish industrial activity was being financed by long and short term credits advanced by great American and European banking houses.

It was reported that in late 1929, thirty technical agreements were signed with big American companies for lending their know-how to the advancement of Russian industrialization. Among these were Du Pont de Nemours, Radio Corporation of America, Ford, Stuart, James & Cook, General Electric, etc. At the same time Soviet purchases in the United States, mainly heavy industrial machinery and equipment, had reached the sum of $109,000,000.

Now, a brief excursion back into Russian history will reveal that receiving help from foreign countries or foreigners was not originated by Stalin's regime. But the Russia of the past was not threatening to spread its ideology and system of government over the face of the world and destroy all forms of society unlike its own. Indeed, today Russia's Premier Nikita Khrushchev is still brandishing his rockets and threatening to crash down the temple of Capitalism—as Samson of the Old Testament crashed down the temple upon the heads of the Philistines.

Foreign skills and capital went into the development of most of Russia's early industries—Belgian money and skill into coal and iron mining; French into mining and metallurgy; British into oil and gold mining, and German into varied other industries.

Russia today is a giant, a formidable world power, buttressed by the governments of at least five East-European, Communist-controlled countries. Military might is based on industrial power, and if Russia is considered in most Western circles as an awesome Frankenstein, it should be recalled that Capitalism contributed substantially to creating it. Premier Khrushchev now is hinting that he has a portfolio full of lucrative orders for Western industrial equipment—and Western businessmen are scrambling over one another to do business with the Kremlin.

Of course, Russia's rapid post-war recovery was due in great measure to the stripping of huge amounts of industrial material from Germany, plus the great heavy-industry base that the Japanese had built in Manchuria which was acquired by Russia as a war trophy.

Russia's industrial strength and scientific capability surged forward so rapidly after the war that the Soviets were the first to put two artificial satellites (Sputnik I and Sputnik II) into orbit in the single year of 1957. Russia's spaceship Vostok I also carried the first human being into orbit around the earth in 1961. These were achievements requiring first-class industrial and scientific ingenuity.

It would be small-minded and transparently envious to deny that the Russian people have reaped many material benefits from their country's great economic development. They have better schools, medical services, hospitals and other public services than they ever had before. But old Russians have told me that they had more democratic freedoms under Czarism than they have been permitted under Bolshevism.

And I am inclined to believe that with the great economic and constitutional advancement that Czarist Russia had begun making from the early part of this century down to World War I, the country might have made just as great, if not greater, progress under an enlightened Czar. If so, the Russian people might not have had to sacrifice so much in blood, sweat and tears.

Totalitarian leaders and governments, from Napoleon on down through Mussolini, Hitler and Stalin, seem inescapably to be expansionist. When I arrived in Russia, the state frontiers were static and embraced about 8,170,000 square miles, with a population of approximately 160 million. Now, as my residence was coming to an end, expansionism had swallowed up 13,000 square miles of eastern Finnish territory, 72,000 square miles of eastern Poland and the three Baltic states of Latvia, Lithuania and Estonia, and Bessarabia and northern Bukovina had been forcibly detached from Roumania. The country had expanded to 8,348,000 square miles and had increased its population to 190,000,000.

This expansion continued even after World War II. Thus, 12,617 miles of the Carpatho-Ukraine were acquired from Czechoslovakia, the 64,000 square mile Tannu Tuva Republic in Central Asia was swallowed up, and southern Sakhalin, 13,935 square miles and the Kurile Islands, 3,944 square miles, were also annexed.

In the summer of 1946, my decision was reached. I accepted a position working in the Editorial Department of the English section of the Ethiopian Government's Press and Information office. I could continue to write for AP and the Negro Press from Ethiopia and most important of all, as a foreign correspondent, the Russians could not very well place any obstacles in the way of my leaving the country to take up a new assignment. Marie Petrovna was another matter. She was Russian and exit visas just were not given Russians to go abroad, not even the wives of American correspondents. The assumption was (and is) that the people belong to the STATE.

I felt, and my good friend the Ethiopian Minister to Russia agreed, that I could do far more in Ethiopia to get my wife out than I could do if I remained in Russia. And with less danger to me personally.

So it was that on an early winter day in October, 1946, I went to the Intourist office in the Metropole Hotel and arranged for a passage on the Russian ship Sestrorets, leaving Leningrad in November.

The time passed quickly. Marie was to retain the apartment, two simple rooms with sky-blue walls. Like all Russian women, she worked, but I left her a solid backlog of rubles, so that money would not be a problem when the time came for her to leave. Fortunately, there were no children at that time to further complicate the situation.

A little farewell party was held in the apartment on the day of my departure with only Marie Petrovna and her two brothers and sister present. After the party, they accompanied me to the railway station. There were hugs, kisses, a few tears and vows and determination to meet again.

Next day, the ship glided slowly away from its Leningrad pier, with an ice-breaker slicing a channel through the ice packs in the Neva River toward the Gulf of Finland. The sky was gray, the air frigid. Thick mists rose from the icy water, soon shrouding Leningrad from view. I left Russia through the same window that I had entered on a brilliant June day in 1932, fourteen long and eventful years before. Perhaps the gloomy atmosphere hovering over my departure carried some symbolic meaning.

Postscript

ON MY WAY TO ETHIOPIA I wrote back from Finland, Sweden, England, France and Egypt asking my wife if she had received an exit visa. She had not. After I arrived in Ethiopia, I barged into the Russian Embassy and gave the Ambassador a sharp piece of my mind—in Russian, too, so that he would understand me fully.

"When I married my wife there was a widespread campaign in Russia lauding the family as being the basis of society," I told him. "What about my family? Or is it only Russian families that are the basis of society?"

He was very sympathetic and correct, assuring me that he would do all he could about having an exit visa issued to my wife.

I sent off resolute letters to Stalin, Molotov and Vyshinsky protesting the withholding of an exit visa to Mrs. Smith. Of course, they did not reply to my letters of protest—I did not expect them to; all I wanted to do was to let them know how I felt about my wife not being given an exit visa.

She recalls: "Waiting for my exit visa was like a shipwrecked sailor waiting on an island for a rescue ship to arrive—it may and it may not. Every time I went to the visa office to inquire, the answer was always the same: 'We know nothing yet. No decision has been reached.'

"Waiting, waiting, waiting for month after month—that's all I could do. And showing too much eagerness would not have been helpful. But I felt assured that my husband was doing everything possible.

"Just as I had almost given up hope, one day they called me to the visa office. 'Your exit visa is ready.' I could hardly believe it; I was almost overcome with exultation—after the long exhausting wait. At last I would be able to rejoin my husband.

"I lost no time in booking a plane ticket and packing my things. I was in a hurry because I was afraid the officials might change their minds for some inscrutable reason."

Something happened—I don't know what—but one day I received a telegram in Addis Ababa from my wife telling me she had been granted an exit visa and was on her way. She would take the earliest plane out of the country for Teheran.

But then oil and politics, a highly explosive mixture intervened. Russia had been negotiating for an oil concession in northern Persia. But Persia had refused to grant it. Relations became strained between the two countries. Aeroflot, the Russian civil airline abruptly stopped flying to Teheran, and no other airline flew into or out of Russia in those days.

Nevertheless, my wife got started and flew to Baku, Aeroflot's southern terminus inside Russia, near the Persian border. From there she booked passage on a small boat across the Caspian Sea to the northern Persian port of Pehlevi.

At Baku, before boarding ship, the Russian customs officials would not permit her to take out her gold jewelry or diamonds. She had to surrender these, with the promise that they would be sent to her relatives in Moscow. That was in 1947, the gold jewelry and diamonds had not reached the relatives in Moscow by the summer of 1963.

Marie Petrovna reached Ethiopia from Teheran and joined me for a residence in Africa that was to last until 1962, when I returned to my native land and brought Marie Petrovna and our two children to what is for her the Promised Land.

INDEX

(top, left) Group of Americans who took part in *Black and White* film project. (center) Catherine Pushkin, great grand-daughter of Alexander Pushkin, Russia's great Negro poet. (below) Robert Ross, Marie Petrovna, Vera and Lloyd Patterson. (top right) Frank Goode, Paul Robeson's brother-in-law. Map showing Maidanek and other extermination camps in Poland. (center) Robert Robinson (below) Ruben Tynes, son of George Tynes, Robert Ross, George Tynes and wife. Ross and Tynes were expatriates.